Seven Decades:
A Learning Memoir

Gary R. Gruber, Ph.D.

Abiquiu, New Mexico

DEDICATION

T his memoir is dedicated to my father and mother, role models and spirit guides, Eugene J Gruber (1912-1979), and Cecil Ketring Gruber (1913-2008); to my children, Martha, John, Jem and their mother Linda, my partner of 35 years; to Ted, Lissa, Rock and Deen; to their mother Susie, who is my current life partner, soul mate, best friend, critic, and co-pilot; and to our twelve grandchildren whom we share with so many others who love and cherish them. Finally, I want to acknowledge my teachers both in and out of the classroom. They gave me a lifelong love of learning that continues to fuel my curiosity about the world in which we live and how we can all work together to make it better, safer and healthier.

"Most of us seek quantum leaps in our performance levels by pursuing a strategy of incremental investment. This strategy simply does not work. The land of excellence is safely guarded from unworthy intruders. At the gates stand two fearsome sentries – risk and learning. The keys to entry are faith and courage." Deep Change: Discovering the Leader Within , Robert Quinn (p.170) Jossey Bass 1996

Table of Contents

Preface

I don't recall anything particularly exceptional or unique about my past seventy-five years. In fact, in most respects, I would say I have had a fairly "normal" and fulfilling life, but perhaps *that* is unusual for many people. As I have listened to the stories of others over the years, I would also have to say that I have been fortunate to have had a rather happy childhood as well as the many opportunities given to me.

I hope that I have taken advantage of enough of those opportunities and learned how best to help others along the way. In my current work, I continue to help others as a coach, counselor, consultant, and teacher, to help them realize more of who they are and what they are about in both their professional and personal lives.

By way of clarification, as it has been, at times, confusing for some people, I am not Gary R. Gruber, PhD and author of SAT (Scholastic Aptitude Test) preparation books and materials. He lives in California. I am Gary R. Gruber, PhD, and I live in New Mexico. While we know of one another and our respective careers, we have not met nor worked together. In fact, I am not a fan of either the SAT or most of the programs designed to help students score better on tests.

In June of 2011, I was invited to give a TEDx (Technology, Entertainment, Design) talk in Redmond, Washington, on the topic of "Learning." TED is a nonprofit organization dedicated to "ideas worth spreading." TED talks are limited to eighteen minutes. I chose to use my seven-plus decades of lifelong learning and highlight watershed experiences from each of those decades. The prerequisite I placed on myself was that the event expanded or changed what I thought, what I did or what I believed. This learning memoir is an expansion of that discourse and includes numerous other learning experiences in each of those decades from the late 1930s through the first decade of the twenty-first century.

Imagine the end of the Great Depression and the ramp-up to World War II. That is when I entered this world. The impact of those two events influenced my childhood more than I could have imagined, affecting both my learning and my life. The Great Depression gave my family values that have stayed with me; and the war, besides capturing everyone's attention and participation, moved me toward antiwar positions later on.

Each of my seven decades has provided me with significant learning experiences that have shaped and formed me into the person that I am today. My awareness of those events and my deep participation in them contributed significantly to my beliefs, values, choices, and my professional career. For fifty years, I have worked as an educator, community activist, and change agent. My review of each of those decades has shown me that my learning was not merely incremental but often radical in that it shook the ground on which I stood. It also awakened me to the enormous possibilities that lay ahead. At times, I encountered significant conflict, dissension, and opposition. At other times, life was calm, peaceful, fulfilling, and joyful. I am most grateful for all those experiences that have given me opportunities to learn, to grow, and to change.

At the conclusion of my most recent decade I have learned what works, what doesn't, and what the critical variables are in the success equation. And it has taken me back to the beginning. I call it the full circle of success because of both my observations in the war years in the '40s as well as my most recent experiences helping others to succeed in their own work and professions. It's rather simply stated, yet challenging to accomplish unless you can persuade talented others to join you along the way. *The success equation is the combination of common vision, common values, and common purpose.* During the war I noticed that the U.S.A. was successful as a result of that fusion of vision, values, and purpose providing a united front. We could still provide a unified front, if we only had the will and the commitment to connect the divisions in a community or a country. As a result of that belief and practice, I have spent my life working to help people to discover passion and purpose beyond themselves.

If we are to succeed in our families, schools, businesses, professions, and elsewhere in our country, we must learn how to build collaborative energy; listen carefully to what is and what is not being said; ask questions that are penetrating and honest; discern the real from the superficial; and help a group move forward with a purposeful, shared vision. Whether it is a small group of committed individuals or a large movement of thousands of people, the aforementioned practices are relevant, valid, and well tested over time. Margaret Mead was *spot on* when she said never doubt that a small group of thoughtful, committed people can change the world, for indeed it is the only thing that ever has. Think of the far-reaching effects of a large group of people mobilized by common purpose and passion, some of which we have been privileged to witness in this past decade. The revolutions of oppressed people in many countries stand as both testimony to the possibility of change and its enormous cost that often includes the loss of many lives.

Our journey as lifelong learners reveals who we are as human *beings,* not simply human *doings.* When we speak of *passion and purpose beyond ourselves,* we need to know what the implications are and how we can realize more of our humanity, our own individual and collective purpose. I believe that this realization has enormous power to effect growth and change that are both real and lasting.

What is most interesting to me is how much has changed in all of these years and how very much has remained constant. I know that I have changed, that I continue to learn and grow and change, and yet much about me is still the same. It's a paradox. The definition of *paradox,* according to the literal Greek translation, is not just *an apparent contradiction* but rather that which is *contrary to public opinion.*

I have often found myself in conflict with the status quo as well as with the private opinions of others. I often went against the grain, swam against the current, and resisted the tide of prevailing public opinion to not only survive but to actually thrive. I have been blessed with the gift of time to learn through experience, dialogue with others, and my own study, questioning and drawing my own conclusions.

The mistakes I have made are mine alone, and I accept responsibility for my errors in judgment that were hurtful to others. I have learned a lot from my mistakes and failures, and I hope that I will not repeat them. George Santayana is credited with the saying that those who do not remember the past are doomed to repeat it

What I have tried to do in these seven decades of learning is to benefit from what I have learned and to help others in their own learning. I have worked in families, including my own, in schools, in communities, and in other organizations and settings. My motives have been mainly to help others, not to achieve any great measure of success, fame, or fortune but rather, as Albert Schweitzer summed it up, to help life where you find it. That aphorism sums up one of my operating principles, and in spite of its overuse on the backs of the infamous Walmart blue vests that read, "How may I help you?," their intentions and motivations are vastly different from mine. Walmart aims to move merchandise, and I aim to *move* people.

When one is *moved,* there is a notion of change, hopefully forward. We can remember the past clearly while moving on, having profited from it by learning those life lessons that will serve and support us in the future.

Chapter One

The Early Years: Listening and Learning

There was a grade crossing (highway road) on the railroad between my two sets of grandparents' homes, and there were no flashing lights or gates, only a wooden X sign that said, STOP, LOOK, and LISTEN. That sign was the same in the small town near one of those grandparents, and it was the same railroad track that went through the countryside and crossed several roads. The train usually blew its whistle far in advance of the crossing, but not everyone had the same acuity of hearing. It was on that town crossing that a train killed one of my grandparents' neighbors and good friend. It was enough to make me, as a young child, somewhat apprehensive and most respectful of railroad crossings and fast trains.

Consequently, this first chapter is about listening and learning, becoming aware of oncoming dangers, and paying attention to adults. I learned a lot from them by just watching and listening, by listening to myself, and by learning from my experiences. That is still true, seventy-five years later. Listening carefully to others is a wonderful learning experience, not only in terms of what is revealed about the others but also very often in the content of what is being said. However, one needs a good filter to separate the relevant information from the meaningless palaver. The same is true for what follows here. You be the judge.

I was born in 1937 in a small, western Ohio town of ten thousand people. Greenville, Ohio, is a county seat that was then primarily a farming community in Darke County. It was one of those small towns where people knew each other, and there was a tremendous amount of community interaction and support. Most of my graduating class of 165 stayed fairly close to home. My wife says that my hometown where I spent my first 18 years reminds her of a Norman Rockwell painting with manicured lawns and white picket fences. So be it.

As World War II approached, tensions increased due to the actions of governments in Europe and elsewhere. As a child in the early 40's, I became aware that everyone seemed to be participating in a national mobilization. Everyone was tuned in and connected to what was happening at the highest levels. This mobilization was palpable, not only because of Uncle Sam and all the visible reminders of who we were as a united country but also because of our shared, common concerns.

We were speaking with one collective voice—politically, economically, socially, and morally. Today we are a much more divided and polarized country, if not fractured completely. Those divisions were minimized during the 40's. We were able to speak with one voice, prevail, and win wars in both the Pacific and European theaters, even though we did so at a tremendous cost and loss of human life. It was called the supreme sacrifice, giving your life for your country. This was the price of our freedom.

I experienced firsthand the air raids and blackouts, and I remember that the only light in our house was that coming from the dial on the Zenith table model radio. Civil Defense (CD), on the home front was practiced regularly, but I do not remember ever being afraid. These blackout drills forced people to practice their responses to the air-raid alarm signals—a series of loud, intermittent siren blasts. Air-raid wardens supervised the drills, standing on nearby street corners with their CD helmets and armbands, making sure no blade of light escaped the houses in their neighborhoods. I did not fully understand why we had air-raid drills in western Ohio, as we were not close to either coast, but apparently it was a national practice. Maybe my town did it because we were close to some manufacturing plants and Wright-Patterson Air Force Base, which was about thirty-five miles away.

These civil defense drills were planned by the local authorities in advance and announced in the newspaper. The streetlights shut off at the scheduled time. Anyone outside was to take cover inside. People in their homes pulled down the blinds on their windows and kept the light inside to a minimum. People in cars pulled over and found shelter in the nearest buildings. The idea was that enemy planes couldn't target what they couldn't see, and that any light visible from above could attract bombs and gunfire.

I did not know and do not remember being told why we did this. It was simply an accepted practice. The federal government sponsored public service announcements to promote participation in the drills and make sure that people knew what to do. Among the more unusual of these promotions was the 1942 song by Tony Pastor and his orchestra, "Obey Your Air Raid Warden," which instructed listeners,

Don't get in a huff.
Our aim today is to call their bluff.
Follow these rules and that is enough.
Obey your air-raid warden!

One popular poster depicted the emergency supplies every household was supposed to have on hand: fifty feet of garden hose with a spray nozzle; one hundred pounds of sand divided into four containers; three, three-gallon metal buckets (one filled with sand and two with water); a long-handled shovel with a square edge; a hoe or rake; an ax or hatchet; a ladder; leather gloves; and dark glasses. Being prepared and equipped for an impending disaster seems like one more thing to worry about that may or, more probably, may not happen. However, preparedness continues to be a big piece of our culture, and being well-defended against foreign invasion seems to be a high priority, considering our huge defense budget. Notice the word "defense."

In my town, no plane spotter ever saw an enemy plane. There were many false alarms however, and many unnecessary blackouts. Still, the air-raid defense effort had to be considered a success. Americans appreciated being asked to take responsibility for protecting themselves, and the opportunity to participate directly in the war effort boosted their morale—which was the actual goal in the first place. I can now see this as a way in which government propaganda manipulates people, although in this case they had seemingly good intentions.

My father, who signed up to join the Navy but was rejected because of flat feet, served as one of those civil defense wardens. I can still see him wearing his white helmet with the red, white, and blue CD triangle on the front, and I was proud of his role in helping to "defend" our country.

By early 1943, there were about six million volunteers in such public protection roles. Two of my uncles served in the military, one in the Army the other in the Navy. One uncle, married to my Dad's sister, was in a tank during the war that was hit by a mortar. He was the only survivor, and though he never spoke about it, it was clear that it affected him for the rest of his life. He lived for another ten years after the war and then succumbed to liver cancer. Another uncle, my mother's brother, went to the Great Lakes Naval Training Center and was stationed stateside. Friends of my parents returned after the war with stories that ranged from terrible suffering and tragedies to heroic actions that saved lives.

As kids, we tried to emulate these men and reenact parts of the war by "playing army." We dug foxholes and tunnels and pretended we had an enemy. We threw dirt clods as if they were grenades. We were trying to do what we had seen in the newsreels: blow things up! We simulated the sound of explosions, and unfortunately I do not have the expertise to recreate those sounds on paper.

The United States actually stopped making automobiles from 1943 until 1946 so that all of those resources could be poured into our military. The assembly lines put together tanks and trucks and equipment needed for a force the world had never seen. And because so many men were taken out of the workforce and drafted into the military, I saw the birth of Rosie the Riveter as women went to work where only men had been previously. I learned then that women could do everything that men could do, and sometimes a lot better, as Ginger Rogers proved with Fred Astaire by dancing backward and in high heels. Women's work during the war was not referred to as "women's liberation," as it was anything but that. They not only had to continue their home responsibilities but they had to work in the factories, usually paid less than their male counterparts.

As a child, I was certainly not aware of the Manhattan Project, but I became acutely aware, in August of 1945, of an atomic bomb and the beginning of the nuclear age. We saw many pictures in newsreels and learned about the bomb during radio broadcasts. Much has been written about Robert Oppenheimer and others who were involved with that experiment. Now, living less than an hour from Los Alamos, New Mexico, the work that went on there and that continues to this day in secrecy is quite interesting. A recent book, *Area 51*, by Annie Jacobsen, raises many questions about government secrets. Whether or not her assertions are all factual, there are certain unanswered questions about which the government either claims no knowledge or will not admit if they do know.

I remember well when the end of World War II was announced over the radio and in the newspapers. We rang the bell in the church on the corner so fervently that it became stuck in the belfry. Someone had to climb up a very steep, high ladder into the belfry to free it. I enthusiastically volunteered, but, alas, I was deemed to be too small for the job, and someone older and stronger was chosen. I determined right then and there that I would get bigger and stronger!

From 1944 to 1951, I took piano lessons, or piano lessons took me, and every week my mother would cart me off to Sylvia Welbaum's house on Martin Street. I had to practice at least thirty minutes every day. My teacher recommended an hour, and my mother reminded me daily to fulfill that expectation. Each week at my lesson, Mrs. Welbaum would listen to my progress on whatever piece I was working on. I don't think she was ever quite satisfied with my performances, and I recall that the last recital for all her pupils was a dismal experience for me. I did learn a few things about classical music and enjoyed being able to read music and play the piano, but not for other people. Each year, I also received a small, white plaster statue of a composer with whom I was familiar—Beethoven, Bach, Liszt, Schumann, Tchaikovsky, and Chopin.

Being well prepared does have its benefits, which I discovered when I eagerly joined the Boy Scouts in 1945. Thus small wonder the origins of the Boy Scout mottos: "be prepared" and "learning by doing." In other words, the Scouts are trained to be in a state of alertness and openness, two qualities imperative to developing into successful personalities and successful leaders, too. Lord Baden-Powell, a British army officer, started the Boy Scouts in England in 1905. Even our local organization resembled a military unit, complete with uniforms and rank. I advanced through the ranks, even becoming a Patrol Leader in my Boy Scout Troop #194! I am not at all sure I fully recognized the transparent connection between the Boy Scouts and the US military forces. The Scouts, complete with camping trips, hikes, and merit badges seemed like fun. The military seemed like a very heavy, serious, and dangerous proposition. The Boy Scouts, on the other hand, were adventuresome! We were probably being brainwashed without even knowing it.

I got my first paying job and my Social Security card at age ten. Consequently, I learned the meaning and value of working for someone else, showing up on time, and how challenging physical labor can be. My first job was to manually set the pins in a bowling alley. This involved sitting high up on a bench above the "pit" (to avoid flying pins); hopping down once the first ball had come through; picking up the pins and replacing them in the rack; waiting for the second ball; hopping down again; and then, with all the strength my ten-year-old arms could muster, pulling down the rack to reset it. Real money for real work!

Our family, along with many others in our community during the war years, had a Victory Garden. By growing our own food those supplies produced commercially could be sent to our armed forces. We saved tin cans and newspapers; reuse and recycle was the mantra long before plastic and the current practice of separating the trash. One of my grandfathers had a shoebox on a shelf in his garage that was labeled, "pieces of string too short to save." When it was full of short pieces of string, he tied them all together, made a ball of string, and used it to wrap packages in brown paper bags. As products of the Depression, my grandparents and parents used and reused everything. Two of the many sayings around our house were "waste not, want not," and "a penny saved is a penny earned."

We were also a do-it-yourself family. When my parents wanted more space, rather than move to a larger house, my dad built an addition of two rooms to the back of the house. One of them became his office and a study, and the other was a laundry, a half bath, and an all-purpose room just off the kitchen. That addition provided a convenient flat roof just outside my bedroom window, which, a few years later, made late-night escapades a lot easier.

If our house needed to be painted, my father collected all the necessary equipment and supplies and climbed up the extension ladder to give our house a new coat of paint. I recall him listening to baseball games on the radio while he painted, and on one or two occasions, he asked me to help, either by running errands to get some supplies or to bring him a cold drink. I don't ever recall his asking me to paint. Maybe he thought I was too young or inexperienced or just wasn't interested. I had a lot of other things to do, people to see, and places to go. I had a set of neighborhood friends, and we were busy building forts and clubhouses and riding bicycles all over town and beyond.

I knew both sets of my grandparents intimately, and they contributed significantly to my early development. Their occupations allowed me to acquire experience both working on a farm and in a general store. I learned the value of meaningful and productive work in each of those very different environments. From my dad's parents, the farmers, I developed a love of being outdoors and close to nature. From my mother's parents, who ran a general store, I was introduced to retail and wholesale, profit and loss, managing a business, as well as a generosity of spirit and substance. From both sets of grandparents, I learned to appreciate the value of an extended family support system. I am sure there were times when I tested their patience and understanding, but what I recall is that they seemed to have confidence in my abilities to learn, to be useful, and to enjoy what I was doing. They were also willing to give me lots of hands-on learning experiences, even allowing me to make mistakes and learn through trial and error.

My paternal grandparents, Eldon and Lizzie, were both born within a few miles of each other in Preble County, Ohio, near a village called West Manchester, and moved to a small farm about fifteen miles from my home. With the exception of electricity and gasoline, which they used sparingly, they were relatively self-sufficient. Because they were so near, I was able to visit them regularly and spend lots of time with them. They had grown up without electricity and indoor plumbing. I remember the day that my dad's parents, the farmers, brought the toilet from the outhouse *into* their house. Truly, it was a day of celebration for *all*. Now, ironically, we're looking for new ways to compost sewage and take it back to the land. Perhaps this is an illustration of what goes around comes around. The raw sewage was first outdoors, then it was taken indoors, and now composting toilets takes it back outside.

I was also privileged, if you can call it that, to see firsthand the butchering of chickens, beef cattle, and pigs. I learned how these animals could feed several families, including our own. My grandfather had a smokehouse where hams and bacon hung from the rafters, and the smell of that shed lingers in my memory to this day. This is but one example of how certain aromas connect us with our past.

The farm was a place for exploration and discovery. I wandered along a stream or field every season. I had an immense amount of freedom, and I spent hours watching and catching crayfish and tadpoles, sometimes wading in the shallow parts, *all on my own*. On more than one occasion, during the wintertime while testing the ice, I fell into the frigid water and had to sheepishly walk all the way back to the house with frozen pants, which thawed out in the toasty warm kitchen by the wood stove. That made the slip through the ice almost worth it.

On this classic family farm, home to cows, horses, sheep, pigs, chickens, and fields of corn, hay, wheat, and oats, I saw neighbors helping one another when it was time to harvest or butcher. My grandparents gave me a variety of jobs that ranged from feeding and caring for animals to driving a tractor. At the end of the day, we sat down to a harvest meal, a veritable banquet of home-cooked and baked goodies of all kinds. Scrumptious!

I walked and ran through the fields. I helped with baling hay and straw and putting it up in the barn. I learned even more about the meaning and value of hard work: planting, cultivating, harvesting, and, ultimately, reaping the rewards. There was plenty of food grown for the animals, and the animals were sources of food for the people, and the people ate well. My family had a strong work ethic, and I received a healthy dose of it early on.

My paternal grandmother, Lizzie Siler, was one of six children, and I knew all her brothers and sisters. While there are many stories, I remember one that continually threw me into gales of laughter, although I am sure no one was laughing at the time. Their extended family owned and operated a furniture store/funeral parlor, the latter being in the back of the store. Because of this, they had the only ambulance in town.

Thus they were required to transport people to and from the hospital when necessary, fourteen miles away.

On one of these trips, Uncle Raymond, who often helped out, rode in the back while enjoying his "chaw" of tobacco. He often found it necessary to open the back door of the ambulance to eliminate the "residue." On one occasion, he, along with his spittle, went flying out the door. The ambulance had to make a quick U turn, retrieve Uncle Raymond from a ditch, and deposit him, along with the original passenger, at the hospital.

On the other side of the family, were my maternal grandparents, O. E. and Jessie Ketring. I was privileged, at the young age of nine, to be given, what seemed to *me* the enormous responsibility of stocking shelves and actually *waiting on customers.*

As you entered the store and looked to the left, you would see shelves filled with canned goods; on the right, running the length of the store, were a variety of dry goods, including fabrics, and a wooden thread cabinet containing spools of every color imaginable. Shoes and boots were in the back as well as the refrigeration and the fresh meat counter. Also in the back of the store was a rack of fresh eggs, brought in by farmers who used them to trade for groceries. The candy counter was in the front of the store, and I would inevitably make a beeline for it whenever I entered the store.

To this day, I wish I had salvaged the big, wooden sign above the store that said, "O. E. Ketring, General Merchandise." I learned later, through the genealogical efforts of one of my sons, that O. E. stood for Orlando Ernestus. It's strange to think I did not know that as a young boy. My grandmother called him Orly.

I learned how to use a gun for target practice and hunting. One day in November, when the cornstalks were down, my father took me rabbit hunting. He carefully explained how to use the shotgun safely and how important it was for certain rules to be followed. I listened intently. The ability to have a gun and learn not only how to use it but also all the safety features and how to care for it seemed like a very grown-up privilege.

One day, as we were walking through the field hunting, he stopped suddenly, leaned down, and quietly said to me, "See that rabbit sitting over there underneath the cornstalk? It's not fair to shoot it while it's sitting, but we'll give it a fighting chance. I'll throw a clod of dirt to scare it out. You give it about a ten-yard head start, aim in front of it, and make your shot."

He threw the dirt clod. Unintentionally, he *hit* the rabbit, and it jumped straight up into the air. When it landed, I shot. I couldn't wait for the ten-yard head start. It was my first lesson in patience…with many more to come. My father showed me how to field dress the rabbit. I proudly put it in the back pouch of my hunting jacket, and I truly felt like I had arrived at some station in life. I just wasn't sure which one or what it all meant.

My parents were born, grew up, went to school, got married, and started their life together in Preble County, Ohio. It was a world of many farms and small towns. My mother and father were married shortly after they graduated from Monroe Township High School in the early thirties. They began their life together in one of those small towns, West Manchester, where they operated a butcher shop and grocery store. From that position, my father was offered a job as a salesman for the Westerfield Brothers' wholesale grocery company in Greenville, Ohio. They supplied similar small stores in a four-county region. They moved to Greenville, and that is where my brother and I were born and where I spent the first eighteen years of my life.

The warehouse of the wholesale grocery company was a three-story building with a freight elevator that hauled the merchandise up for storage and down for packing and shipping. What I remember most were the cases and cases of everything from cereal to condiments. The aromas of the various spices permeated the entire warehouse. I also remember the space where orders were assembled, wrapped, and labeled for delivery. There were several large trucks that delivered the orders to the various retail grocery stores, and I was sometimes lucky enough to ride along and help with deliveries.

My father once brought home a case of Renuzit spot remover when I was about ten years old. He suggested I sell it door-to-door in the neighborhood. He sold it to me for his wholesale price, and I was to sell it for the retail price. I quickly learned a few lessons about salesmanship, the retail business, and profit margins. My overhead was very low and there was no advertising budget. I believe I only sold one case before I gave up. And what did I learn from that? I learned what I didn't want to do. I really did not want to be in the business of selling anything.

Following World War II and with the advent of large grocery store chains, many of the small mom-and-pop operations went out of business, and the wholesale grocery company soon followed and was liquidated. A similar pattern with the big box stores continues right up to the present day.

My brother was born in 1941. Being four years younger, we did not do a lot together in those early years, although he was along for our many family trips. Visiting the big cities of Dayton and Cincinnati to see relatives and taking in sites such as the Cincinnati Zoo, Coney Island, and Crosley Field was a big deal for a child in the forties. On one of those trips, I learned how to change a flat tire. Even better, on another trip, I watched Jackie Robinson, the first African American in major league baseball, play second base for the Brooklyn Dodgers. I did not quite understand at the time what the big deal was just because he was the first. I thought the hoopla was more because he was such a good player.

My memories of the 1940s are of the war, of my family's hard work to ensure our survival. I have memories of going to church, of a small, cohesive, supportive community of friends and neighbors, of great independence to explore the world in which I lived. There were many family gatherings that ran the gamut from Sunday dinners on the farm to a long bus trip to California in 1942 with my mother, brother, and grandmother in order to "escape" a polio epidemic. Travel on trains and planes during the war was reserved mostly for military purposes, thus the bus.

We made the same trip by car in 1947 in a brand-new Oldsmobile, complete with hydramatic drive, one of the earlier automatic transmissions. It was dark green, and I put stickers on the windows of the many places we visited en route. Conoco gas stations supplied some of the decals, and I picked up others at various souvenir shops along the way. We carried a canvas bag of water in case the radiator of the car boiled over in the heat while we crossed the desert. My mother's sister, Edna, a lovely woman, lived in Salinas, California, and she was the primary reason for those California trips. I learned later that she had become pregnant by my grandmother's brother-in-law, who was my aunt's uncle by marriage, and that they "ran away" to California to have the baby.

Church played an important role in my family's life, and many of my parents' friends were members of the same congregation, the First Congregational Christian Church on West Fifth Street. From an early age, I was expected to attend Sunday school in the basement along with a hundred or more other kids, all divided by age and grade level. We sang hymns, listened to Bible stories, and then trotted off dutifully to our classes. As if that weren't enough, we were then expected to endure an hour's worship service upstairs in the sanctuary.

During one such service, when I was nine years old, I noticed the church ushers passing large brass plates along each row of pews into which people were putting envelopes and *real* money. I looked up at my father and whispered to him, thinking this might be a way to pick up a little extra money, "Could I take some out?"

Looking at me with his characteristic wisdom and candor, he said, "Yes, you may take some out, but remember always to put in more than you take out."

I didn't know it at the time, but that characteristic piece of sound advice from my father would serve me well for many years.

I learned more outside of school than inside of school. I learned from my family, from working with local shopkeepers, and summer experiences on the farm.

My mother made sure that I had a lot of opportunities to expand my horizons, and she was a constant source of encouragement and support. Whether teaching me how to garden or cook or even clean the house, she knew that these skills would come in handy later. She also made sure that I got connected to other things outside of home, such as the Scouts, summer camps, community events, and a familiarity with life beyond our local community. My mother was a great organizer of family trips, vacations, social gatherings with other families, and she exhibited a positive and happy personality to all who knew her. She went back to work to help pay for my college expenses and to give me other opportunities for travel and recreation. My mother was a great role model of generosity and gratitude as well as a no-nonsense approach to work. She gave of her time and energy to many causes that she believed worthwhile, such as her church, other volunteer activities, and helping those less fortunate.

The church I attended sent me to a camp one summer. Camp Chaffee was in a rural location about forty miles away. It gave me a typical summer camp experience. I slept in a cabin with counselors, followed a daily schedule, shared in the work chores of meals and cleaning up, and met new kids and adults. We sang songs, played games, learned folk dances, and made things such as baskets and pottery. The church part consisted of spending time alone in the morning, supposedly reading the Bible or praying or being inspired by nature and being close to the God of creation. I seemed to get more out of the meditation part than following a set schedule. However, some of that early discipline must have left an impression on me, as demonstrated by an early career choice.

Like many young boys of that era, I had a paper route; in fact, I had two different routes at different times. The first was with the *Dayton Daily News*, and I recall that the Sunday edition was almost too big to handle on my bicycle, so either my mother or father would assist by driving me around my route in the car. That aid was especially welcome in bad weather. The other route was for the *Greenville Daily Advocate*, a much smaller, local newspaper that I could throw from my bicycle, hopefully *directly* onto the porches or steps of the customers' homes. It was important to reach the target, because to leave a paper in the bushes or too far from the door meant a call and a complaint.

School seemed easy, and with little effort I learned one could get good grades by doing well on tests, giving the right answers aloud, and generally pleasing the teachers. I can still recall the names of every teacher I had from kindergarten through twelfth grade. At some point, around second or third grade, I remember being interviewed, along with my parents, about advancing a grade, and I remember my parents saying no to the proposition. It didn't matter to me very much one way or the other. Now, I think they made the right decision.

I started my school career in kindergarten in a room in the back of a building called Memorial Hall. I don't remember much except the naps on the rugs, the smell and taste of that white paste from the big jar, which we spread with a tongue depressor, and listening to stories read by the teacher. I began first grade in the South Elementary School where Lillian Ongst prevailed. She was a loving, caring, kind, soft-spoken teacher—very encouraging and supportive. She had a son named Harold and spoke of him often. She seemed proud of his accomplishments and probably wanted to inspire us to reach for greater things beyond first grade. So I reached for second grade in the same building with Hazel Fry. She seemed quite serious, and it was clear that we were there to work, and her job was to make sure that we were successful, in all subjects, no matter what it took. The basics came easily. Reading, writing, and arithmetic were rather enjoyable, and I treated them like a game. Her son was an accountant, and she was committed to making us all competent mathematicians. She also wanted to make sure we had the required skills to advance to the next grade.

We moved from one part of town to another during my second grade year, so in third grade, I attended East Elementary School. These novel and creative names emanated from their locations in town. The school you went to depended upon where you lived. Interestingly enough, there were only three elementary schools; there was no school in the western part of town.

Mabel Snyder was my third grade teacher, and she seemed like a reprise of Mrs. Fry. She was serious, dedicated to her craft, concerned for each student's good work, patient, and persevering. I'm sure both Mrs. Fry and Miss Snyder smiled more than I remember, but it didn't bother me that they didn't tolerate much foolishness from any of us. At least once a week, Miss Snyder must have said, "You are here to *learn*, not to fritter away the day just playing around."

In fourth grade, I moved upstairs in the old East School into a large, sunny room with large windows and an outdoor, steel, fire escape. Edna Hartle was our teacher, and she taught us with great charm, grace, and a sense of pleasure and satisfaction. She was a stately woman, had great posture, was well dressed, and smiled a lot. She seemed well organized, had a plan for each day, and, because she enjoyed what she was doing, she expected that we would, too. For the most part, we did.

My fifth and sixth grade teacher, and also the principal of the school, was Lowell Bowers. For at least several of those years, he ran the local Dairy Queen during the summer. His forte was math, and although that was not my favorite subject, he persevered, as did I, and we got along just fine. During my sixth grade year, our school building was condemned, as it was slated for demolition, and we had to move to the junior high school a year early.

I am often surprised that I remember those teachers so well, and I have obviously forgotten more than I remember. I remember much more about their characters and personalities than the content they taught us. What I do know is that each of them exerted some kind of positive influence over me and instilled in me the value of learning beyond just doing the work. Their commitment was apparent, and regardless what they might have said to each other or what complaints they had about the system, they gave us lots of learning opportunities, and for that I remain extremely grateful. In the years that followed, I learned to value teachers far beyond what they taught. As I moved into the field of education myself, my admiration and respect for my teachers increased exponentially.

The junior high school and high school building was my home for the next seven years. I had met my wife-to-be in the fifth grade when she drew my picture for the school newspaper, *The Keyhole*. She must have done a fairly decent job and impressed me favorably, because we dated off and on during high school and then progressed to "going steady."

She lived two blocks away, had two sisters, and it was easy for us to become part of each other's families.

Our junior high and high school were housed in the same three-story building, a block from my house. A classic school building of the 1930s, it had large windows in every room that opened into a central hallway, so all the offices and classrooms were on the outside perimeter of the building. The gym space took up two of the three stories, and the locker rooms were underneath. The junior high/high school sat on the western side of a city block, and in the middle was St. Clair Memorial Hall, a large theater complete with stage and even a few classrooms on the second floor and industrial arts and auto shop in the basement. The Carnegie Public Library sat on the eastern side of that large city block. This made for a "campus" feel, and it was definitely the community center for many activities involving both young people and adults.

The basement of the library housed someone's collection of taxidermy, which mostly consisted of local animals as I recall. There was an assortment that included a squirrel, rabbit, pheasant, and groundhog. There were various large and small birds, a mounted fish or two, a beaver, a bat, a fox with a big bushy tail, an opossum, and a skunk. The whole place had an unpleasant smell, and it wasn't the skunk. The animals were old, dusty, and very dead; we loved to touch them. Their fur was very stiff and not at all soft and fluffy. I half expected to see a stuffed cat or a dog, but no such luck.

My parents signed us up for Community Concerts, with the theme, "The Best Is Yet to Come." Community Concerts was an organization that brought musical entertainment to small towns that did not have any local, professional resources in the performing arts. In the 1920s, America underwent rapid change and modernization, and the arts were no exception. While Chautauqua tours, traveling minstrel shows, and vaudeville had created a national appetite for live performance, they were disappearing from the scene. There was a demand for concerts. The question was finding a way to cover the cost.

In 1927, an idea destined to revolutionize the performing arts in America sprang up simultaneously in the Great Lakes region and in several Eastern states. Instead of struggling to make up deficits after the fact, people thought, why not raise the money first and then hire the artists? It was a plan that worked, and it ensured the success of the humble experiments that grew first into a pre-paid, organized subscription audience and ultimately into Community Concerts, the largest, most enduring network of performing arts presenters that has ever existed. The organized audience idea caught fire and spread: it fostered cultural development on an unprecedented scale. Early featured artists included Vladimir Horowitz, Lawrence Tibbett, Jascha Heifetz, and Yehudi Menuhin. I remember in particular a piano duo, with two people playing two pianos. Most performers had national reputations. Sadly, my piano lessons did not propel me to such heights of performance.

Although the stock market crash of 1929 threatened this brave experiment in the arts, Community Concerts continued to grow. People were determined that economic hardship would not deprive them of beauty and meaning in their lives. Meeting minutes from local Community Concert Association meetings held in Dust Bowl towns refer to families who could not afford the fifty cents to attend the concert and were being carried by loans from neighbors or by the Association itself.

After World War II, Community Concerts expanded rapidly. Between 1945 and 1950, the total number of Community Concert Associations rose to an all time high of 1,008. Community Concert Associations were formed in Canada, Mexico, the Caribbean, and even, briefly, South Africa.

Chapter Two

Schooling Is Not Education: Learning Beyond the Walls

T he 1950s was a decade of schooling: junior high, high school, college, and a marriage in 1958. Like Mark Twain, I did not let schooling interfere with my education. I spent a lot of time in school, and I am sure I could have taken much better advantage of it. The progression through school was indeed like the factory model of education. We moved through the assembly line in batches of age groups. We even lined up to keep order. The bell rang, the whistle blew, and we all salivated, just like Pavlov's dog. Conditioned to respond to the authority of the teacher (boss), we went to school (work) and produced correct answers, which were measured by tests (quality control).

In the summer of 1951, perhaps in an effort to keep me connected to the Boy Scouts, I was offered a job by the area council and encouraged to accept a position at a summer camp, Camp Cricket Holler. As a junior staff member, I was assigned to the kitchen crew and was also the steward for the dining room. Imagine a fourteen-year-old in charge of three hundred younger boys three times a day in the dining room and trying to get them to do what they were supposed to do in terms of setting tables, serving food, cleaning up, and maintaining some sense of order and decorum. Between meals, I worked in the kitchen helping to prepare food for the next meal. I learned the value of teamwork, learned that friends would cover for you if necessary, and that I was expected to return the favor if asked.

Dorothy King was the head cook and in charge of the menus, ordering food, storage, and preparation. She taught us how to scramble eggs and prepare breakfast for three hundred hungry boys. We also had the other two meals to get ready every day. The twelve-burner cook stove was in a center island with a large vent hood over the top. One day, one of the young cooks, held the big skillet with one hand and reached up to rest his other hand on the inside edge of the hood. Some kind of electric charge went through his body, and he flipped the entire skillet of freshly broken eggs all over the kitchen as well as the rest of us cooking nearby. We laughed until it hurt and until we all had the mess cleaned up. I believe Dorothy probably said something like, "Well, boys, what did you learn from that little fiasco?"

Dorothy's husband, Larry, was the camp ranger and in charge of all the buildings and grounds and outdoor equipment. Sometimes, he called on us to help him with moving things, cleaning up, and general maintenance projects—all good experience and training.

My paternal grandmother died of a heart attack in 1952. At age sixty-four, she did not seem very old to me. I knew that she'd had a kidney removed earlier, but I was unaware of any serious health problems, as she appeared to be an active farmer's wife. She gardened, tended her chickens, cooked large harvest meals, and managed a very active household with great energy and spirit. She was also the matriarch of the Gruber clan, fifteen to twenty people who gathered periodically for Sunday dinners, holidays, and other special occasions. Domestic rituals were part of her household, including church every Sunday without fail.

Hers was the first death of a close family member, and I watched everyone with great interest as we walked through that experience. Her casket was placed in the formal dining room where people gathered to pay their respects, and I saw my grandfather cry for the first time in my life. We all went to the small church in town for the funeral and then to Twin Chapel cemetery, where many of my family members on both sides are buried. I have visited there several times since then as my mother and father, as well as my three other grandparents, aunts, and uncles, are buried there. I don't plan to be buried anywhere. I choose not to take up precious space in the ground. And what my family does with my ashes is up to them, although I might have a suggestion or two. For example, depending on where I die, the ashes can be scattered into the wind or into the water, as long as I return to the earth from whence I came. I know only the latter part of this quotation from Genesis 3:19, which is: "By the sweat of your brow you will eat your food until you return to the ground, since from it you were taken, for dust you are and to dust you will return."

Another summer job and learning experience came the following summer when the railroad, first the New York Central, and later the Pennsylvania Railroad, was hiring men (and in my case, big *boys*) to rebuild the tracks. Although we were supposed to be eighteen, if we were big enough and appeared strong enough, they seemed to overlook the age requirement and signed us on. I wasn't old enough to drive a car, so I had to get a ride with a friend in order to report for work. Then the railroad transported us to the work site, often a remote spot in the countryside fifteen to twenty miles away from town. We earned $3.25 per hour; for a forty-hour week, that was big money for a fifteen-year-old in 1952. And, if we were lucky enough to work overtime, time and a half pushed the hourly rate even higher. Twice there were train wrecks, which ended up giving us double time at $6.50 per hour. Fortunately no one was hurt. In general, the hours were long and the work tedious.

I worked every summer at something both challenging and rewarding, whether as a laborer on a construction job, a lifeguard at a swimming pool, or a skilled operator on the railroad. Since several of us high school young men were among the few working on the railroad tracks who could read and write and understand verbal instructions, we were given an enormous amount of responsibility operating equipment far beyond our skills and experience. That was a little frightening, but we were excited by the challenge. What I learned was that listening carefully to what was needed helped to get the good jobs, or at least good from our perspective. It seemed easier and more pleasant to sit on a piece of equipment than to wield a shovel, a pick, or a maul. We did our share of lifting ties and rails and lining track but moved quickly into less strenuous jobs operating equipment as the heat and hard labor took their toll.

One job I particularly recall was following the crew and burning the old, rotten railroad ties on the gravel bed next to the tracks. A wind came up and blew some sparks into a nearby farmer's wheat field. The entire field caught fire and burned the crop to the ground. The railroad was held responsible and had to compensate the farmer for his loss. Fortunately, no blame was levied at us, since we were just following instructions. That phrase, "following instructions" or "just following orders," came up later, and I wondered then why we did not have the good sense to either question the wisdom of building a fire so close to that field or to find a way to put out the fire before it spread to the entire field. *Just following orders, sir.* Perhaps we should have trusted our own judgment rather than following orders without question. Lesson learned.

At school, no academic subject particularly challenged me, thus I had a *great* time. I played football, basketball, and ran on the track team and always found time to socialize with numerous friends. I learned how to communicate in writing, with fairly good penmanship, and aloud by speaking in public. And all of this was done without the benefit (or burden) of any electronic device. Even the typewriter on which I learned the basic QWERTY keyboard was manual: JUJ, space, FRF, space. And: "The quick brown fox jumps over the lazy dog," which uses all the letters of the alphabet.

One of my classes, which we called Shop, was under the heading of Industrial Arts. We learned woodworking, how to sharpen and care for tools, and how to make something with our own hands. My creation was a coffee table, the center leg of which was made on a lathe from a bowling pin. Our instructor, Bob Hawes, was missing parts of two fingers, a great object lesson in safety and caution.

I learned to cook with Mrs. Orpha (not Oprah) Palmer. I acted in a play, *Our Town,* by Thornton Wilder, playing the role of Editor Webb, Emily's father, opposite "our" Emily, Sonja Norris, who would later become a nun. I sang in the high school and church choirs and was a member of a boys' quartet. I do not remember having a particularly good singing voice, but apparently it was good enough to make the grade. What I did have, without realizing it at the time, was an excellent liberal arts education, one that prepared me well for later years.

An interesting note about our high school athletic endeavors was that our coaches were of the highest caliber, expecting quality performances based on diligent and thoughtful practice, and they treated us with respect and trust. In turn, we worked hard, had a modicum of success, and benefited enjoyably from the overall experience. The football and basketball coaches in particular seemed to illustrate the maxim that "the harder I work, the more luck I have." The 1954 football season was notable in that we were undefeated, won the league championship, and I earned a place on an all-state team. We may not have been the biggest or the fastest team on the field, but I daresay we were among the best coached. And, of the starting eleven players on the football team, all of us went on to college and graduate school. I figured that, if nothing else, we just played *smarter* than the other teams.

I graduated from high school in 1955, and, at that time, I did not believe I was sufficiently prepared to take on the demands of a rigorous college education. Although I was admitted to a prestigious Ivy League college, I neither felt ready for that experience, nor did I feel socially adept to enter that world. I chose instead to attend a highly rated state university, Miami University, in Oxford, Ohio, about fifty miles from my home. I spent a large part of the summer of 1955 on that campus with other students headed to other colleges and universities, learning *how to study.* The practice of survey, question, read, review, and recite (SQ3R) was indelibly imprinted on my brain. It was a study skills class, and I learned for the first time how to take notes that made sense. I also took courses in English and math that summer and entered Miami University of Ohio in the fall of 1955.

It was easy to go home on occasional weekends, since my father was the general manager of a Ford dealership and gave me a car to use. One incident, during my sophomore year, was particularly memorable. I was driving home with a high school friend and fraternity brother and we both lived fifty miles north of Oxford. Approaching an intersection at about fifty miles per hour, I saw a car stopped at a stop sign. Since I had the right of way, I continued forward. She obviously did not see me and continued on. I swerved but to no avail. My car clipped the tail end of hers, spinning my car around and flipping it on its side into a ditch.

As we came to a grinding halt, I had a death grip on the steering wheel. Remember, there were no seat belts at that time. When the car stopped, I was still sitting in my seat, albeit sideways. I asked my friend, who was curled up in a ball between the seat and the dashboard, if he was OK. Luckily, he was. We were able to climb out and walk to a nearby gas station. The attendant said he had seen the accident and had already summoned the police and an ambulance. Once I realized that my friend, the other driver, and I were unhurt, my major concern was telling my dad. The car had been totaled. I called my father, fearing the worst. His reply? "Do not worry. I can replace a car; I can't replace you."

My girlfriend had gone off to Ohio Wesleyan University a year earlier, in 1954, and she transferred to Miami in 1955, partly so we could be together. The end of my junior year in college coincided with her first year of stewardess training with American Airlines. She discovered that her class was being trained for the first transcontinental jet flights and she would probably be stationed in either New York or Los Angeles, too far away for us to be together. In those days, flight attendants had to fit certain physical and social requirements and were not allowed to be married. She passed all the former requirements but could not sustain the latter one. She ended up returning from Love Field in Dallas, Texas, and we married. She began teaching sixth grade in a rural school with thirty-five students. As a teacher, my wife was paid an annual salary of $3,500. I told her at the time that her salary amounted to $100 per student for the *entire year*.

Our rent in a second-floor apartment over an unclaimed freight store on High Street, in Oxford, Ohio, was $125 per month. We had a budget. Envelopes contained cash allocated to the essentials, which included rent, utilities, groceries, transportation, and entertainment, but very little of the latter.

The beginning of this marriage in 1958 was also a type of schooling; it was an enormous learning experience. I learned a tremendous amount about the value of caring for another person and our children, of the priceless support from an extended family, what it takes to make a primary relationship sustainable and productive, and how to give of one's self and not count the cost.

Those four years at the university introduced me to a more serious engagement with an academic curriculum that allowed me the benefit of choosing some courses outside of my major concentration. I had begun a course of study in pre-med but shifted to religion after my sophomore year. One elective of particular interest was an architecture class called "The House." I learned then, that if possible, you should select a great teacher, regardless of the subject. Professor Charles Stousland, known to his colleagues as "Mik," was one of those teachers. He was stimulating, challenging, inspiring, as well as creative and funny. I seem to recall, in addition to the previously mentioned attributes, he drove a *vintage* Rolls Royce, which impressed me considerably. The course was all about residential design and construction, but it was the *teacher* who gave the course meaning and purpose and enabled our understanding. His explanations were detailed and humorous and the field trips to a variety of architecturally designed houses were fascinating.

I was fortunate to have been exposed to several teachers who inspired me. All of these teachers left a mark somewhere deep within me.

Stan Lusby, Arthur Wickenden, and Richard Delp are three other teachers that I recall. Those instructors, when coupled with my own innate curiosity, gave me an internal push in the direction of teaching and learning. This is illustrated by the fact that I have dedicated fifty years to helping others expand their own awareness of themselves and the world around them through working in a variety of educational environments, either as teachers or leaders.

I graduated from college the following year in 1959, ending this decade of schooling. I looked ahead to even more education, another institution of higher learning with more courses of study, classes, professors, and long, difficult assignments.

Chapter Three

Turbulent Times: Rocking the Boat

T he sixties became known by its own numerical identity and was a defining chapter, not only in my own personal life, but also in the social and political landscape of this country. Its effects can still be seen and felt today. From protests focused on civil rights and a very unpopular war to the nuclear arms race and political activism, this decade influenced an entire generation of people, including today's baby boomers. Many people considered the sixties as radical and subversive, and it was certainly a time when I became much more of a left-leaning liberal. Some people labeled me as subversive and somewhat threatening to the status quo. A left-leaning liberal in a rather conservative community is an easy target for those who wish to discredit, undermine or otherwise reject someone who appears to be in disagreement with the prevailing norms.

From 1959–1962 I attended Princeton Theological Seminary and in the first year, along with many others, I had doubts about whether this was the right place, the right career choice, or the best option for whatever lay ahead. As an alternative, I considered flying for the navy, took a pilot's test at Lakehurst, New Jersey, and passed. I asked if I could postpone flight training at Pensacola and finish my first year at Princeton, and the answer was yes, indeed, I could join the next class.

During that period, before I could enroll at Pensacola, two close friends and former fraternity brothers, were both killed in separate accidents flying for the navy. One, Don Hickman, was killed in training in Corpus Christi, Texas, and the other, A. E. Kemmer, was killed flying off an aircraft carrier in the Pacific when his jet had a flameout. He ejected, but his parachute failed to open. I spent time with his family soon after his death and experienced firsthand the grief the tragedy had spawned. Another friend's older brother, Tom Troxell, whom I knew well, from my hometown, was also killed in a plane while flying for the Marines in California. The messages seemed clear. Why put myself in such a high-risk position? While flying seemed both adventurous and attractive, the statistics did not seem all that favorable. I decided to keep my feet on the ground, stay at Princeton, and finish the course there.

I drove a bus for Tiger Bus Lines, later to become Suburban Transit, during my stint at Princeton to help make ends meet. On one of those occasions, I took the Princeton Glee Club to New Haven, Connecticut, to sing at Yale in a joint concert. We stopped at a Howard Johnson's restaurant on Interstate 95, and upon leaving a state highway patrolman pulled the bus over. In a private conversation, the officer told me that apparently some of the boys had taken some salt, pepper, and sugar shakers from the restaurant. He asked me to let him handle it, and he stood in the front of the bus and announced to the boys, "It appears that some of you forgot to leave some salt and pepper shakers at the restaurant. I will pass through the aisle with this bag, you put them in and no further questioning, OK?" I admired his tact and diplomacy as well as his generosity, thanked him profusely, and we continued our journey with the delinquents in silence.

During those three years at Princeton, I discovered that I did not especially enjoy learning Greek and Hebrew, although both were required for graduation. Reading and interpreting the original texts was a grueling experience, and since so many scholars had already done it already, why were we required to do it all over again? Theology and philosophy were more interesting, and some of the readings and lectures were intellectually stimulating. We read works from Paul Tillich, Karl Barth, and Reinhold Niebuhr along with other giants in the field who led the way for reformed theological thought and understanding. Their insights regarding theology seemed to connect to contemporary social issues, and it was easier to believe in the practical application of those systems than some of the more ancient and historical writings. Theology for me had to be relevant to what I was experiencing in my daily life. It was only later that I found value in some of the more ancient literature, although I realized even while at Princeton that it had significant historical value. Church history itself was also interesting, and when I understood the social sources of denominationalism a lot of things fell into place that had very little to do with religion itself and more to do with economics, geography, parity, and one's position in the community.

Paul Scherer, a professor of homiletics, interpreting scripture and preaching, said something that I will always remember. Who knows why *some* things that teachers say stick and most things they say don't? Dr. Scherer encouraged us by saying that that we were "to comfort the disturbed and to disturb the comfortable." That resonated well with my own values, and I remembered to employ it often, at least when I thought it was appropriate. I tried to balance that equation, although I am certain that those who received either the comfort or disturbance thought otherwise.

As I was about to graduate from Princeton in 1962, I accepted an appointment as an associate pastor at a church in New Jersey that was founded in 1717. With revolutionary war soldiers buried in the nearby cemetery, this was a bona fide life lesson in United States history. Those who sacrificed their lives for their beliefs helped launch this country. History tells us that it often takes a revolution to achieve independence and freedom.

Nineteen sixty-two was also the year of the Cuban missile crisis and John Glenn's orbit around the the earth. It was also the year that James Meredith became the first African American to enter the University of Mississippi. It was the year of the Beatles, Bob Dylan, and the Beach Boys. It was the first year that Walmart and Johnny Carson appeared. Another Carson by the name of Rachel launched the environmental movement with the publication of *The Silent Spring*. All of these cultural icons and many more made a deep and lasting impression on me at age twenty-five. However, the most significant learning experience on the personal front was the birth of my first child, a daughter, in December of 1962.

On August 28, 1963, I learned from Martin Luther King, Jr. in his famous "I Have a Dream" speech, that if we were to live in a country where people were going to be judged by their character and not by the color of their skin, I was going to have to *do* something. It was not enough to simply listen. It was one of the first times I recall asking the question about the discrepancy between what we *know* and what we *do*. There seemed to be a gap between what we knew to be true and what we were willing to do because of our knowledge or beliefs.

In June of the following year, in Mississippi, Medgar Evers, a civil rights activist, was murdered. Shortly after his murder, three civil rights activists were lynched at midnight on June 21, 1964: James Chaney, a twenty-one-year-old African American from Meridian, Mississippi; Andrew Goodman a twenty-year-old anthropology student from New York; and Michael Schwermer, a twenty-four-year-old, also from New York. From that point on, the movement intensified and accelerated. The Civil Rights Act in 1964 was a piece of landmark legislation, but it became clear to many of us that morality cannot be legislated.

Forty-one years later, in 2005, the perpetrator of this horrendous act was finally convicted.

Our first child was one year old in 1963, and I started on the journey of learning how to be a good parent and how to help a community and a society pay attention to issues of diversity, equity, and social justice, which had kept us segregated, even after the Civil Rights Act of 1964. We moved to suburban Detroit in 1964 where I accepted an appointment at a very large, all-white, suburban church in Grosse Pointe Michigan. I was given the freedom to work in the community as a social activist. In 1967, there were riots in Detroit, and we were placed under a curfew. Once again, I learned the meaning of a blackout, but this time it was not a fear of bombs but a fear of civil unrest and more violence that kept us in the dark. I protested segregation and advocated for integrated housing, employment, and education. I also protested against a very unpopular war in Vietnam. Our two boys were born in Detroit, in the fall of 1964 and 1968, respectively, and as my community responsibilities increased, so did my family responsibilities.

During the curfew, we were supposed to be off the streets and at home by 10:00 p.m. One night I was visiting with a friend six blocks from my home. I realized it was close to 10:00 p.m., and I thought I had better start home. My friend encouraged me to stay a while longer, mentioning that it would be all right, that I wasn't far from home. I agreed and stayed on past 10:00 p.m. As I was ready to leave, I noticed the streets were dark, and there was absolutely no traffic. I was violating curfew. Should I leave my car and walk quietly through the shadows or should I risk taking the car and quickly traveling the six blocks undetected? I opted for the latter. I inched slowly down the street, lights off, and as I turned the corner of our one-way street, large searchlights from a military vehicle bathed my car in bright light. As I pulled into my driveway, uniformed soldiers escorted me out of the car, put me against the car, and searched me, supposedly for weapons. I felt something like the barrel of a gun in my back, and I froze as I realized my own freedom had just been compromised. It was a sickening thought and feeling, one that must have been felt many times by so many others in similar situations, guilty only of breaking a rule that may have seemed irrelevant and unnecessary.

Protest has an interesting history and is the root word of Protestant. In the early sixties, I had studied civil disobedience as illustrated by Martin Luther, a German pastor, and Mahatma Gandhi. Luther's 95 theses were written in 1517 and Ghandi led the protest against the national salt tax in 1930. I learned even more about World War II and the Holocaust. German pastors Dietrich Bonhoeffer and Martin Niemoller were associated with protesting the Nazi imprisonment of Jewish men, women, and children. They were among my numerous heroes and models for social justice. I then met Martin Luther King Jr. in Detroit in 1968. As a member of the board of the Grosse Pointe Human Relations Council, I was involved in inviting King to come and speak to a mostly all-white audience in the suburb of Detroit. I was in charge of arrangements at the local high school, as it was the only venue large enough to accommodate the anticipated crowd. The atmosphere was extremely tense. Many police groups were present, including the FBI, the Michigan State Police, and the local police department, who had jurisdiction. A heavily armed squad of police stayed quietly and secretly in the school library in case there was any kind of trouble. From the local police squad, Lieutenant Sylvester was in charge, and he was my direct contact.

As the capacity crowd assembled, Lt. Sylvester and I watched people come into the auditorium where plainclothes police positioned themselves strategically throughout the crowd. As King was introduced and began to speak, hecklers in the crowd attempted to interrupt him by shouting loud enough to sufficiently draw attention to themselves and away from King. I told Sylvester to get those people out or there could be trouble. He asked if I would be willing to sign the complaint. A quick debate ensued, as I thought that was his job, but I finally agreed, just to get some action. With a few whispered words into his lapel microphone, some of the plainclothes policemen escorted several protesters out of the auditorium. King, showing amazing patience and understanding, continued his speech concerning the moral imperative of equal rights for all people, regardless of skin color.

What I did not know at that time was that the protesters were taken to the local police station and booked under some law related to disturbing the peace or creating civil unrest, and that *my* name appeared on the charge. That, in turn, led to my being labeled and attacked by several right-wing groups, including the John Birch Society.

It would be another decade before I would meet Elie Wiesel, author of *Night and Dawn* and several other Holocaust survivor tales. I learned from Wiesel that "to remain silent and indifferent is the greatest sin of all." He helped me understand the moral responsibility of all people to fight hatred, racism, and genocide.

During that time in suburban Detroit, I helped design a course for high school students that focused on human sexuality. I was an organizer and an active participant in the Grosse Pointe Family Life Education Council and was asked to teach a human sexuality class at a nearby private school. Although the class was controversial, as were many other issues of the times, I agreed. To avoid public criticism from such right-wing groups as the John Birch Society, we gave the course the euphemistic title of "Life Planning." All tenth grade students were enrolled in the class, which met twice weekly, and we covered many topics that were relevant to these fifteen-year-olds, including an attempt at increasing their understanding and appreciation of human sexuality. I had become acquainted with Mary Calderone, the noted outspoken advocate for sex education, who, at the time, was the executive director of the Sex

Information and Education Council of the United States (SIECUS). She was a tremendous resource and source of encouragement. It was she who first suggested I consider going on to graduate school in the field of family studies.

The Family Life Education Council (FLEC), invited Haim Ginott to speak to the parents in the community about effective parenting. He had authored the very popular book called *Between Parent and Child*, published in 1965. His genius was capturing the meaning behind children's words and deeds. He spoke in front of a fairly large audience and at one point suggested that parents should treat their children more like *guests* in their homes. He gave the following example: If a guest spilled a glass of milk, your response as a host would not be to get terribly upset or make some critical remark but instead help the guest by cleaning up the spilled milk. One parent commented that he would start *treating* his children like guests in his home when they started *acting* like guests in his home.

By the spring of 1968, I had been a community organizer and activist for five years and had helped plan an appearance of Dr. Martin Luther King Jr. who was to speak to a primarily all-white audience in suburban Detroit. That gave me the opportunity to spend two days with Dr. King during his visit. One month later, April 8, 1968, he was assassinated, and I learned that personal sacrifice was a high price to pay for your beliefs. With my own safety and that of my family threatened with harassing letters and phone calls because of my very public role in the community, I dropped out of the movement in 1969 and escaped to the idyllic hills of central Pennsylvania with my wife and three children. I enrolled in graduate school for the second time around. During my time in suburban Detroit, I had also served on the Boards of the Franklin Settlement House, the Northeast Child Guidance Clinic, as well as the Grosse Pointe Human Relations Council. I learned that one way of contributing to a community is to get involved in organizations that serve and support activities that I believe make a difference in the quality of life for all people, especially children.

I looked closely at three different university programs: the University of Minnesota, the University of Connecticut, and Pennsylvania State University. These were the only places that offered graduate studies in human development and family studies at that time. I selected the College of Human Development at Penn State University and their program in Individual and Family Studies. Mary Calderone had given me an introduction to Carlfred Broderick, a professor in Family Studies in the College of Human Development at Penn State. He and Dr. Joe Britton, chairman of the department, persuaded me that Penn State would be a good choice.

During my time at Penn State, I had the good fortune to participate in several research projects and learned about the stages of early childhood development, adolescence, and human growth over the life cycle.

We had moved to central Pennsylvania in the summer of 1969. I drove a bus again for some extra money. I drove mostly charter trips, not only for the university but for other local groups as well. I also worked at two rural churches in central Pennsylvania on Sundays, one in Spruce Creek and the other in Sinking Valley, about four miles from Spruce Creek geographically and a hundred miles socially and politically. Those small family-oriented communities were about a half hour's drive from where we lived. Spruce Creek happened to be one of Jimmy Carter's favorite trout fishing places.

The bus company I worked for was Fullington Auto Bus, and it made a regular run over the mountains to Lewistown to meet the train. This work gave me the experience that allowed me to work, during the seventies, for Arrow Bus in East Hartford, Connecticut, and Connecticut Limousine, experiences that I still remember with pleasure to this day. The opportunities to travel to new places, see the sights, and get paid while doing so, seemed to me to have many advantages. And to this day, I still enjoy driving our own "bus" in the form of a motor home across the highways and byways of North America.

The first twenty-five years of my life laid down a strong foundation to enjoy and endure the next fifty. Consider what your first twenty-five years contributed to your learning and your involvement with your community and the larger world. In my own case, that first quarter century was defining, and much of it endured over the next fifty years and is still resonating in different ways.

Chapter Four

Turning Inward:
"The Me Decade"

The seventies seemed to be a reaction to the turbulent and troubled sixties, and many people withdrew from being political and social activists; I know I did. The novelist Tom Wolfe, writing in *New York Magazine* in 1976, described American's preoccupation with self-awareness, with the phrase, "The Me Decade." The article was entitled "Me and My Hemorrhoids," and I found his reflections both very descriptive and quite amusing.

In the 1970s, I shifted gears professionally and moved from teaching children to teaching adults. I worked in schools, universities, and hospitals where I had the benefit of observing even more about human motivation, human development, and human behavior. I learned about organizational development and how systems worked and learned why sometimes they didn't work. A system worked because it was designed with the users in mind and involved them in the development and application process. A system often didn't work because it was pre-fabricated, imposed on the users, and was not tailored to their specific needs.

My course of studies as a graduate student in the College of Human Development at Penn State University would last four years and result in a master's degree in child development in 1971 and a doctorate in family studies in 1973. Those years in State College, Pennsylvania, "Happy Valley," as they called it, were indeed happy. We rented a small cottage on the outskirts of town. Since we had come from the Detroit suburbs, where children played on well-defined sidewalks and driveways, our children were at first puzzled by all of the space.

Our youngest child was just learning to walk, so he was occupied with that developmental task, along with numerous others, but the older two were sufficiently independent to entertain themselves and discovered a whole new world outdoors with no sidewalks but replete with fields, trees, and animals of all kinds. We left that environment after three years and moved back to a suburb, this time near Washington, DC, so that I could write my dissertation and do an internship. The children had to make the adjustment back to sidewalks and driveways. I learned that children, as well as their parents, could be very flexible, adaptable, and rise to the challenges.

During our stay in State College, there were numerous occasions of delight and discovery, whether with the children or with friends in the world of antiques and country auctions. In fact, during my three years on campus, I did not attend one football game, preferring instead to visit those farm auctions in the valleys between the mountains, often with good friends.

We acquired numerous items of interest, including painted blanket chests, textiles, decorated stoneware pottery, and some other period furniture, including a couple of Windsor spindle back chairs. We also became interested in printed frakturs, or birth certificates, printed in German and decorated by hand. For a short time, we had a corner in a store in Boalsburg called The Country Sampler. My wife and I had great fun buying and selling antiques, traveling around to different markets and shows, and sharing a common interest.

Our oldest son, John, intrigued by Ranger Rick and other natural venues, was discovering an entire world outdoors to his great pleasure. One day, however, he was sitting in old truck, pretending to drive. Unbeknownst to him, a swarm of bumblebees had built their nest under the seat. He came running into the house in tears, his bottom covered in bee stings. He was, hurt and *surprised*. He told us, "I tried to be their *friend!*"

I did numerous projects in graduate school, two of which stand out in my memory. One concerned student activism on college campuses. Three of us were assigned to write a trilogy on the topic. One person took the personality of the individual student, another the culture and climate of a particular college or university, and I researched the family backgrounds of the students involved. There were no big surprises or revelations, other than what one might expect, that set the stage for students who took an active role in protests. Students who espoused the values of free speech and who actively opposed suppression or oppression by political or other institutions were willing to go to the wall for what they believed. My own research showed that the families of these students held similar values regarding social justice and peace but were surprised when their sons and daughters took them at their word and actually acted on those values, even at the risk of being arrested or putting themselves in serious conflict with authorities. I recognized that dynamic very well. I had been in similar positions in the previous decade as a civil rights and antiwar activist.

The second project concerned young children who were exposed to high levels of violence on television and its effects on aggressive and prosocial (friendly and desirable) behaviors in those children. This research project received national attention and was followed up in other universities and endorsed by Action for Children's Television (ACT). What I saw and heard convinced me sufficiently that violence as portrayed in the media *does* have negative and deleterious effects on children's behavior and possibly on adult behavior as well, which would have been another project. One of ACT's major successes was the passage of the Children's Television Act of 1990. Shortly after the passage of this act, Peggy Charren, one of the founders of ACT, announced the closing of Action for Children's Television, suggesting that it was now up to individual citizens' groups to police the airwaves. Although there may be a greater awareness, there still seems to be more than enough violence portrayed in the media, available to all regardless of age.

Once I completed my course of study, internship, and dissertation, I was faced with the challenge of choosing *what* I would do, *where* I would do it, and *why* I would do it. There seemed to be three fairly distinct options. With a family that included three young children, their needs were also one of the important variables in my career choice equation.

One possibility lay in teaching at the college or university level but having had a taste of that with all the departmental policies, politics, and university expectations of continuing research, it was the least appealing path. I was more interested in practical application than in theory and research. It was also a time when federal funding for university research had been cut dramatically. What I have learned since is that practice should inform theory and not the other way around. Theories that had not been field tested for validity did little to advance the practice, which seemed to me to be a lot more important than the theoretical precepts. It also seemed that there was a ten-year lag between theoretical research and its practical application. Maybe that was because the research had to be proven to be effective before it could be adopted.

Another choice was to go to work with an existing community group, such as a mental health clinic, a social service agency, or a hospital. Again, the political climate of many organizations seemed more problematic and negative than positive and constructive. I had already worked in several different types of groups, so I chose not to pursue that kind of association.

A third choice was to become an independent practitioner of family systems. In any event, my experience pushed me more in the direction of working in the field rather than the university classrooms and laboratories. My experience as a private practitioner was most affirming.

With that in mind, we decided to relocate to Lancaster County in Pennsylvania once my internship in Washington was finished. We had lived there for several years and knew we liked the area. I began a private practice in counseling and consulting with an emphasis on helping individuals, couples, and families deal with issues of conflict that troubled them personally and in their relationships with others. I decided to give it a year and project what I thought would be sufficient to continue or move on. Within six months, I was able to support my practice and my family. My community-focused activities with schools, hospitals, and other local social service agencies continued for seven years, from 1972–1979. A number of people have remembered my work there. Recently one woman, now in her fifties, recounted how I had helped her when she was a young child. She had to confront a most difficult relationship with her distant father, and through our work together she was able retain a modicum of self-esteem that helped her overcome her fears and insecurities. She has gone on to a very responsible and productive life.

Compared to the 1960s, I found Americans in the 1970s were for the most part self-absorbed and passive. They turned from street theater to self-therapy, from political activism to psychological analysis. We called it "navel gazing" as groups of people sat around exploring their inner selves and sharing some of their deeper feelings, which ranged from anger and fear to excitement and hope. The challenge was to get people out of their heads and into their emotions. Numerous self-help groups were established to help people express themselves and deal with emotions that were often in conflict with either their families or themselves.

There seemed to be some differing opinions between the cognitive theorists and the behaviorists and I thought I had to choose which I was going to adopt in my own practice or which made the most sense. One eminent researcher, Candace Pert, author of *The Molecules of Emotions* finally made it clear in her work My own personal (and professional) view is that we can distinguish thoughts from feelings, and while both may well be part of the same system, the mental or cognitive realm can be as distinct from the emotional state of being as the physical condition can be from the spiritual experience.

Some did not believe it was possible to separate thoughts from feelings. Actually there was some element of wisdom in the group work as opposed to one on one individual work, as research has shown that people learn much better in groups than alone. That was to have even greater implications later on, as students in schools were asked to "do their own work" when in fact they work and learn better in groups, working together on meaningful projects.

The problem is that in schools, where *everyone* went to learn, we were taught to do it on our own. If we copied someone else's work or if we gave the answer to someone else, it was called cheating. But in the real world, working together is called collaboration, and finally, after forty years, this concept is working its way into our schools.

What I learned in the '70s was to start asking others, and myself *why*? Why are we doing it *this* way? Is it just because that's the way we have always done it? As I began teaching and learning again, this time in graduate and post graduate programs, I had the opportunity to work as an instructor for teachers and physicians who were hoping to educate their own students and patients. The teachers were helping their student learn what would support their success in their work and lives and the resident physicians were helping their patients learn how to be healthy and take care of themselves.

Almost everyone in the seventies, it seemed, had an analyst, adviser, guru, genie, prophet, priest, or spirit guide. In the 1970s, it seemed like the only way many Americans could relate to one another was to be a member of a therapy group, seeking some form of healing and mental health.

I'm OK, You're OK by Thomas Harris was on the bestseller list for two years in the early '70s. I rather liked the tongue-in-cheek follow-up called *I'm OK, You're Not So Hot* by Dolph Sharp. I learned that therapy wasn't the cure-all it promised to be, and that if anything were to carry the day, it would have to be personal responsibility.

I recall reading a book, the cover of which was in black and orange, called *Trick or Treatment: How and When Psychotherapy Fails* by Richard Stuart. There was one particular chapter that stayed with me called, "The Iatrogenic Effects of Dispositional Illness," and it dealt with the negative effects of labeling. His idea was, and it still rings true for me, that sticking labels on people yields very little in the way of positive results. However, the insurance companies all demanded it, and when I was an intern in Washington, DC, we played the insurance game with the *Diagnostic and Statistical Manual of Mental Disorders*, DSM III (now V), which was the classic definition of mental disorders used by practitioners to satisfy the insurance companies. We would sit around a conference table and decide, based on our observations, what *label* to give someone in order for them to collect the insurance. However, while labeling someone as neurotic or obsessive-compulsive, or anxious did little to change their behavior or solve their problems, it solved the insurance problem.

Around 1974, Dr. Nick Zervanos invited me to teach a course at Lancaster General Hospital for third-year residents in family practice. The title was "The Doctor-Patient Relationship," and the goal was to get these young doctors to focus on the person and not merely the presenting problem. Instead of a doctor saying he has a "foot" in room three, my task was to insist that the doctor refer to the person by name, such as, "Mr. Johnson is in room three, and he has a problem with his foot." The whole person was in room three, not merely his foot.

I used videotapes taken in the treatment rooms of clinics, with the permission of the patients of course, for feedback to the physicians. They would frequently come back to my station where I was watching several rooms simultaneously and ask how they were doing. When I mentioned to Dr. Levine that Mr. Jones had mentioned money three times and Dr. Levine had not responded once, he gave me a look of shock and surprise. Whenever I asked the young residents if they would like me to play these moments back to them, they often said, "Yes, but just please don't use it in class!" Ah, the MDeities, as we liked to joke with them. Doctors playing god did not impress many who worked with them on a daily basis.

It seemed like so much activity in the seventies was focused on relationships, and the high priest was the psychologist or the psychiatrist. We all ended up in some form of therapy, learning how to be in touch with our inner selves and manage our emotions. It still rings true that much in life is about relationships, either those between individuals or between individuals and groups or between one group and another. How we make those relationships effective and productive, positive and constructive is often hard work and, at the very least, takes sufficient time and energy to nurture and support. Learning to navigate the parent/child connection as well as husband/wife, employer/employee and many other critical relationships including teacher/student and citizen/government requires enormous inner resources and resilience and sometimes patience and forbearance as well. And of course, lest we forget, *forgiveness*.

In the early seventies, we purchased a house as a fixer-upper to remodel and sell for a profit. It was a story and a half cottage on South Prince Street in Lancaster, Pennsylvania, for which we paid $5,000. We did some work on it and sold it for $10,000. It wasn't enough for a down payment on another house, but every bit helped. I learned that with a little creativity and ingenuity, one could make a wise investment as long as there was sufficient preparation, background research, and some hard work to go along.

At the time we were renting a duplex, half of a large farmhouse, just south of Lancaster. The owners were a Mennonite family who owned and operated two large dairy farms. I was able to work part-time on the farms to help pay the rent and found the work enjoyable and reminiscent of my earlier days on my grandparents' farm in Ohio.

On the same day that I purchased a hindquarter of beef and had it cut, wrapped, and frozen, my wife announced to us that we were to become vegetarians. That was somewhat illustrative of one of us thinking and going in one direction while the other was going 180 degrees in the opposite direction. However, we managed to bridge the gaps, at least for the next several years.

The children had started school. Two of them attended Lancaster Country Day School, and the youngest, Jem, attended a nearby kindergarten in Lampeter, PA. Jem sometimes turned the J around so that it looked like an L, thus his name appeared in print as Lem rather than Jem. His teacher asked him if he wanted her to call him "Lem." He replied, with a degree of bravado, "I don't care *what* you call me; *that's* how I write my name." His early sense of autonomy and independence only grew stronger as the years went by.

In an early conversation with nine-year-old Jem, I reminded him, "When I was your age, there was *no* television."

He, obviously shocked, said, "There has *always* been television!"

I responded, "Yes, in *your* lifetime but not in mine."

He then asked me, most curiously, "Dad, when you were my age, were there *cars?*"

I must have seemed very old, but I told him that indeed, "I was not *that* old," and "Yes, cars were very much around throughout my life."

The other two children had their distinct personality traits as well, and what is interesting to me is to see how some of their early characteristics have also grown stronger and become manifest in their adult lives. For example, the oldest of the three was clearly a take-charge kind of person, ordering her two younger brothers into compliance on numerous occasions, and they obediently did as their big sister told them, at least *most of time*. The second in line, John, was the proverbial middle child, the mediator, kind and gentle, seeking to help the others whenever possible. Today, at their current ages, they still exhibit these early traits, perhaps in different venues, but they are quite apparent to me and to others as well.

We moved from the country into our first house in town. We borrowed the down payment from my father at a very low and favorable rate of interest and got a mortgage from the Strasburg Bank. The cost of the house, a three-story, four-bedroom townhouse built in the late 1800s and in the historic district, was $65,000. It required some cosmetic improvements but was soundly built and structurally in good shape. After being renters for seventeen years, buying a home felt like an important milestone in life's journey. Setting goals and moving toward them deliberately, consciously, and intentionally is a practice that works well in many instances. There is much more to that process than merely having a goal. Having some kind of plan about how to get there helps enormously.

In 1979, my father died. He had been a tremendous influence in my life. When I got word from my brother that he had died suddenly of cardiac arrest, my world was temporarily turned upside down, not only because it was unexpected but because he was a relatively young and healthy man of sixty-seven. My mother's first words were, "I knew that this day might come, but I never thought it would be this soon." She mirrored my own thoughts and feelings perfectly.

I recalled having talked with my father about his father's death. I had known my grandfather and loved him very much. My father had used that occasion to talk with me about the inevitability of his own departure from this earth some day. He shared his thoughts about life and death and how he had tried to make the most of his life and added he thought I was doing the same. That was a difficult conversation but typical of my father's style of using life experiences to illustrate and say something about his own personal values and beliefs. He had written a letter, detailing all the arrangements in the event of his death. When that day arrived, everything was in order, just as he had said it would be.

A year later, on the anniversary of my father's death, we made a point of having my mother with our family. We noted his passing, remembered his life, and shared stories. My mother said, at the time, that since they had been married for forty-five years she doubted that she would get married again. I told her that she was still quite young at sixty-seven, very attractive, and that she shouldn't rule out the option of getting married again. She should be open to finding someone with whom she could share life and enjoy the many things that gave her pleasure. With a bit of a twinkle in her eye, she said, "Well, maybe some day I will eat those words." And sure enough, three years later, my mother married a man whom I had known when I was very young. He and his brother had operated a service station, a Sunoco gasoline station about three blocks from our house. She and Jim Gettinger were married for twenty-five more years before she died at the age of ninety-five, two months shy of her ninety-sixth birthday.

Chapter Five

Computers and the Internet: Is Faster Better?

I n my early years, I learned that the speed of a .22 caliber bullet could cover two to three thousand feet per second. I thought that was extremely fast until I learned later that the speed of light was 186,000 miles per second or 700 million miles per hour, which is about 983,000,000 feet per second. Sound, on the other hand, affected by temperature, humidity, and altitude, travels, on average, around 1126 feet per second. That caused one pundit to say that's why you may think some people are very bright until they open their mouth to speak. It must be the voice that slows things down. It may be true that our minds work faster than our tongues can speak. Therefore, it's helpful to have the mind in gear before engaging the mouth.

With the advent of computers, there was a whole new language to learn that had to do with bytes and bits and megabytes and how fast information is downloaded and uploaded with the help of broadband networks and the Internet. Did I need to learn and understand how many bits were required to spell "cat" or how fast the information might travel using words, pictures, movies and music? I have been and continue to be a Mac devotee, and my answer was, "No, I didn't need to know all the particulars." I just needed to learn how to use the basic on and off switches and how to get started with various applications that allow me to communicate, such as word processing, e-mail, and the Internet. I have learned how to call tech help when I need it, and those good people have usually walked me through whatever issue I was dealing with, whether it was hardware, software, or often in my case, *user* error. With more recent tools such as Google and Wikipedia or the social media networks, more information is available than ever before in history, and it is accessible to anyone, anytime, anywhere as long as you can connect to the Internet.

It was in July of 1980 when Bill Gates met with IBM to talk about writing software for their new PC. He convinced IBM to let Microsoft retain the licensing rights to MS-DOS, an operating system that IBM needed, and Gates proceeded to make a fortune from that business deal.

On November 10, 1983, at the Plaza Hotel in New York City, Microsoft Corporation formally announced Microsoft Windows, a next-generation operating system. Steve Wosniak and Steve Jobs released the Apple I computer in 1976, and Apple was launched. While it began small in the marketplace, it grew into the giant that it is today.

When I saw the update of the earlier version to the Apple IIe in 1983, I knew it was only a matter of time until we succumbed to a growing interest. In 1987, my son, while still in college, was actually the first in our family to purchase a computer. It was a home-built machine with several separate components all put together by a brainiac in Providence, Rhode Island. A computer of this type was de rigueur for all the "science guys." Since I was *not* a science guy, my first personal computer was a Macintosh Classic, a lower-cost version that I bought in 1993. All that I had to do was figure out how to make it work.

**Simplicity
is the
ultimate
sophistication.**

**Introducing
Apple II,
the personal
computer.**

The opening up of the Internet in 1988 to public use is what unleashed a tremendous expansion of individual and corporate computer use. The Internet had previously been restricted to primarily government functions, such as the National Science Foundation (NSF) and the military.

Some may also remember the early days of Atari, a pioneer in video games and dominant in the computer entertainment industry well into the 1980s. Electronic advancement was not high on my personal learning list, although I understood that these new devices offered great promise for many industries and applications, and for the future. Little did I know what was yet to come and who could have predicted the advent of the handheld devices that now prevail, including pads, pods, and phones, all connected to the Internet. There was tremendous development in the '80s and a conversion to a higher speed network as the net opened to other users. I began to question whether faster was always better? The specter of superlatives reigned large—and this bumper sticker of the '80s summed up the culture of consumption: "He who ends up with the most toys wins."

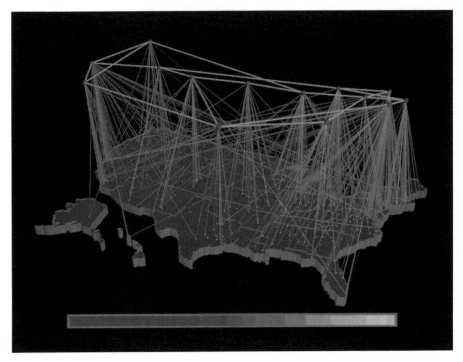

In the 1980s, I learned a fair amount in the early days about how computers work, or I should say, how to *use* computers, because I understood very little about how they actually worked. I still thought sending *a fax* was magic.

The first Apple Macintosh was released in January 1984. From that point on, I was hooked up to a Mac of some kind and am sitting here, almost thirty years later, writing this text on a thirteen-inch MacBook Pro with a Mac OSX 10.7.5, to be precise. It's not the latest or newest operating system, but it's sufficient for my needs. I am convinced that there is an intentional, built-in obsolescence to computers, and that there is a conspiracy of sorts to make us all believe we *need* the latest gadget, whatever it might be. It's all about marketing and sales and profitability.

Watching and listening carefully to all the ads designed to increase our consumption was another learning experience of this decade.

I continued to question what I perceived to be the values that spoke loudly and frequently of fastest, best, most, latest, newest, and greatest. I found myself in conflict once again with our culture of conspicuous consumption, along with the imperatives and superlatives that accompanied the marketplace. The imperatives of spend, buy, waste, want, and borrow were at war with my early training and family values of save, use, keep, have, and give. I am still at war with our culture's values. As I read recently, it's not about consumption, since we are all consumers of just about everything one way or another. It's really about over-consumption, of consuming more than we need and participating in a materialistic culture that emphasizes *things* instead of people and values.

In 1979 I accepted an appointment to become a department chair, chaplain, teacher, coach, and counselor at a college preparatory boarding school in New England, Choate Rosemary Hall. This was an enormous shift for our family, and our three children and I took up residence in Connecticut while their mother stayed behind for a year as we tried to work things out in a fractured marriage. Eventually, she came back to live with us the following year. We remained together for the next fifteen years until a divorce became imminent in 1995.

Choate Rosemary Hall was the result of a merger between the former all boys' Choate School and the all girls' school Rosemary Hall that had moved from Wallingford to Greenwich, Connecticut many years previously. New buildings were constructed "up the hill" from the main Choate campus for Rosemary Hall to return to Wallingford in the early '70s. For a number of years the two schools were coordinated, and then they merged into one school under the leadership of Charles Dey. He persuaded me to join the faculty there as a teacher, a department head, a chaplain, a coach, a counselor, and an adviser. I had the privilege of serving in both the faculty and the administration and regarded Charlie as one of my mentors in school leadership.

Life on the campus of a beautiful New England boarding and day school from 1979 through 1985 was filled with wonderful colleagues, experiences, and relationships. It was here I learned even more about adolescents as we were privileged to be in their company every day. There were almost a thousand of them in grades nine through twelve, and we observed them in a variety of contexts including eating, sleeping, playing, and working together. Not only did I lead a department called, somewhat euphemistically, "Behavior and Ethics," I also taught classes, helped coach football, drove the ski bus to a nearby mountain for recreational (not competitive) skiing, started a program to help a hospital in Haiti, and wrote a book with a colleague called *Understanding and Enjoying Adolescence*. The premise was that if you could understand adolescence better, you could enjoy it more, and we aimed the book at the adolescents themselves, their parents, and their teachers. The book was published by Longman in 1988 and remained in print for ten years.

It was not *all* roses and sunshine. One of several crises that we faced during those years was an infamous cocaine bust in 1984 that made national news. A student had collected money from several other students and flew to Venezuela to bring the cocaine back to campus. Another student quietly informed us of what was happening, so that without any fanfare or public knowledge, we helped the customs authorities intercept the errant student on his return to Connecticut via a New York airport. The fallout was serious. The press covered the story and attempted to interview other students and faculty. However, the school actually survived quite well.

Some of our peer schools contacted us saying that the incident could easily have happened to them, and they asked what they could do to offer support. Others were concerned that this event and the subsequent publicity might adversely affect admissions and a capital campaign. On the contrary, people realized we were serious about a zero tolerance policy, and admissions inquiries increased, and the capital campaign was very successful. This also was the result of excellent leadership at the top.

We learned several important lessons related to community culture and values, public relations, and how to manage a firestorm. It was one of my early experiences in expelling students from a school that "said what it meant and meant what it said." We wanted our students to know that attending such a school was a privilege that one earned, and it was not something bestowed automatically by one's station in life. I was able to draw on that experience, and others there, when I was called upon later to make similar critical decisions, not only related to illegal drug use but other unacceptable and inappropriate behaviors, from bullying to cheating and even stealing. These were hard lessons learned by many students. Some students learned from their mistakes while others did not learn, at least that time around.

In 1985 I was recruited to become the head of an independent college preparatory school in suburban Philadelphia (kindergarten through twelfth-grade). The Shipley School was founded in 1894 by three sisters, Hannah, Katherine, and Elizabeth Shipley, daughters of Murray Shipley, a Quaker merchant who, when he fell upon hard times, told his daughters they would need to find a way to make it on their own. These well-educated Quaker ladies believed firmly in what was then a controversial idea—*education for women*. Their establishment was to be far more than a finishing school. In the fall of 1894, when the school opened with six students and nine faculty members, they established a philosophy of education that would guide the school for over a hundred years, up to the present time.

In their first catalogue, the Shipley sisters stated that it would be their aim "to fit [the student] to enter college with a mind trained to habits of scientific study and a character qualified, in as far as possible, to receive the highest culture." In many ways, the school has remained true to that original mission, and while the names and faces have changed, the ultimate purpose and *raison d'être* have not.

During my seven-year tenure as head, we created a middle school program in addition to advancing the school in numerous ways through continuing admissions and marketing efforts, fundraising, *friend* raising, and establishing the first endowed teaching chair. We made great strides in supporting professional development for faculty and establishing the school as one of the premier private schools in the region. My monthly meetings with other heads of regional schools were among the highlights of my tenure as the head of school. One of the many assets of Shipley was a strong board of trustees with outstanding leadership. When I arrived, Herb Middleton led the board, followed by Sandy Stengel. Jim Jennings played a major role, as did Skip Snyder, Barb Crawford, Bette Peterson, and the president of Bryn Mawr College at the time, Mary Pat McPherson. She was a good friend and neighbor and offered sound and timely advice and support.

On one occasion, my wife and I were invited to dinner at Mary Pat's home along with several others, including the president of Haverford College, the former president of Swarthmore, and other very accomplished educators and community members. The buffet dinner was laid out beautifully—expensive china, sterling silver, candelabra, the works. There were several choices of entrée, including fish, beef, and many other selections. It was a lovely evening with fine wine and good conversations. We stayed late into the night. When we arrived home, upon taking off my coat and tie, I discovered a sterling silver fish knife in my coat pocket where I had placed it while going through the buffet line. The next morning I had my assistant call the president's assistant and explain what had happened and that the knife would be returned immediately. I received a call shortly afterward, and Pat said, "Dr. Gruber, I know you are raising money, but don't you think this is going a little too far?" Having a great sense of humor is in fact a prerequisite to being a good leader.

I enjoyed those seven years immensely, especially the relationships I developed with students, parents, and teachers. They formed a wonderful learning community and embodied the motto of the school on a daily basis, "Courage for the Deed, Grace in the Doing." What better character traits would one want for their children or for themselves?

Courage and grace are a great combination and tremendous resources to have available to call upon whenever needed.

I had a terrific staff of colleagues and formed an administrative team of six who represented the academic divisions, admissions, business, and development. We were known as G-7, and we met weekly to review and plan, to analyze the past, present, and future and develop plans for moving forward. We created, with the help of a much larger group of constituents, a strategic plan that would be a road map to the school's future. The school was grounded in a strong liberal arts education, and the families of the students were very supportive in helping us be successful.

One of the more challenging aspects of being a CEO or head of any organization is being ultimately responsible for what happens there, whether in the areas of personnel, finances, programs, or buildings. There were several challenges.

A particular employee was not behaving appropriately, and suffice to say that the only person who disagreed with that assessment was the employee himself. We terminated his employment with clear instructions that he was not to return to campus. However, he ignored that stipulation and began to visit at unpredictable intervals. I was the one who had to confront him and ask him, as politely and tactfully as possible, to leave without causing any more disturbances. He would leave but then suddenly a week or so later, he would reappear. Finally, after the third or fourth visit, I told him that if he came back again, I would have to call the police.

Obviously this was emotionally upsetting to him, and he began to shout threatening obscenities to me, and for a moment or two I thought I was going to be physically attacked. I began walking away backward, slowly, trying to calm him down, as I did not want to turn my back. When I got about twenty-five yards away, I turned around, kept walking and, looking over my shoulder, I saw him get into his truck and drive away. I returned to a meeting from which I had been called and asked my administrative team, what, if *anything*, did this have to do with the *education* of children? One wise woman, Barbara Zolliker, head of our lower school, said, "Mr. Headmaster, this has nothing to do with the education of children, but it is an *obstacle* to the education of children, and part of your job is to remove the obstacles." I have remembered those words as clearly as if she had said them yesterday.

The postscript to this story is that the employee returned again and parked in front of the school. I called the police, and they came and escorted him away. We were then sued for discriminating against him for his religion, although we had no idea what it was, and the suit was thrown out through the good offices of our attorney.

Chapter Six

Leadership:
Challenges and Rewards:

I n the summer of 1992, I was invited to join a very different kind of school, one that served a thousand at-risk children and had the necessary resources to do so. The Milton Hershey School in Hershey, Pennsylvania, is a story unto itself. I was asked by the president at the time, Fran O'Connor, to take on the academic and residential programs as one of four vice presidents with the title "head of the school". The other three VPs were in charge of finances, human resources, and communications. I saw a challenge that was worthwhile, worth my time, and worth the investment of experience and energy in what seemed like a unique opportunity to have a positive impact and make a difference in the lives of students and adults.

After a year working at that school in Chocolate Town, I realized it was a school of unlimited funds but an extremely limited vision. The level of dysfunction and corruption was hard to fathom and even more difficult to accept. Fran O'Connor was in her first year on the job. She was the first president to be appointed from outside the school and the first woman to occupy the position. Formerly, she had been a successful independent school head in New Jersey. She had asked me to take on this very responsible position of leadership in the school's administration, but she was fired in April before I started work. Thus, I became associated with a person who had been judged unacceptable by the vast majority of eight hundred employees, one-third of whom were related to each other.

I recall Fran telling me that the average tenure of the employees there was *twenty-seven years*. Her comment was, "Do not mistake twenty-seven years of experience for one year of experience twenty-seven times!" Words to live by!

Since the rank and file found it impossible to accept an outsider who had originally been selected in order to plan significant change, how were they going to receive someone appointed by that outsider? My impression was that the board hired her without getting buy-in from the staff. In fact, it turned out that they were opposed to most change, especially when it involved doing things differently. They were a classic case of being wed to the status quo.

The acting president and chairman of the board, Rod Pera, asked me to stay on and continue to help with moving the school forward into the twenty-first century. We began designing a number of institutional and organizational changes, many of which were threatening to a very large group of entrenched employees. The dynamics of making changes in a place that had not changed much in a hundred years were fraught with conflict and disagreement. There was open and organized opposition, dissent, resentment, and resistance to change. Status quo was king, and Milton Hershey was the prince of the realm.

One of my tasks was to interview candidates for the president's position, and I managed to earn a modicum of respect from many people there while I served in the newly created position of director of research and professional development. However, I also believe I was viewed with a degree of doubt and suspicion regarding my intentions and motivations.

The place was rife with fears and insecurities too numerous to mention. There was also a deep pocket of very conservative religious beliefs and practices, and this ran counter to my own position. Employees held a vigil at the gravesite of Milton Hershey during these tumultuous times, and I think they expected him to reappear and save the day.

There were three final candidates for president. They were Art Levine from Harvard, Bill Lepley, a state superintendent of schools in Iowa, and David Hornbeck, an expert in school reform from the state of Kentucky. The board selected Art, and he and I had several conversations about the future of MHS and how we might work together.

Near the end of that year, although I was offered a major leadership position, I determined I could not continue to work in such a toxic environment. One seventeen-year veteran called the school's lavish expenditure of money "a vulgar display of wealth," and I had to agree that although money seemed plentiful, the way it was used and wasted was unacceptable. The budget at that time was around forty-four million dollars annually, and that computed to forty-four thousand dollars per student per year, all paid for by the trust.

One Friday afternoon in New York City, I told Art I was not staying on. He asked why, and I proceeded to give him a long list of reasons that we discussed in some detail. This discussion took place after he had already accepted the appointment as president but before he actually took office. His appointment had been highly publicized, however the following Wednesday he called the board and resigned, which resulted in more turmoil. I was again asked if I would remain, and my answer remained, "No, thank you." The corporate response was, "What would it take?" I explained that my decision was not related to money. Art went on to become the president of Teachers College at Columbia and just recently retired from that position. David Hornbeck became the superintendent of the Philadelphia Schools, and Bill Lepley became the president at MHS.

After my departure, I took another one-year position as interim head of a school in Princeton, New Jersey for the 1993–94 school year. The

Hun School also had a few problems but nothing compared to the scope and scale of Hershey. John Hun, a professor of mathematics at Princeton University, started Hun in 1914. The school initially focused on tutoring students in math in order to prepare them for the nation's top colleges, though it soon expanded into a complete school, teaching all disciplines, and added a boarding department. By 1925, there was space for 150 boarding students and a significant number of day students as well. The number of boarding students has remained constant while the number of day students has increased significantly. The campus has continually expanded and improved, and the school serves its students well in preparing them for their continuing education and life's other challenges.

Committed now to school leadership and reform, I was eager to find a place where I could be creative, contribute to a teaching and learning community, and help people realize their vision and goals, both professionally and institutionally. Knowing that I would be looking for another opportunity after my one-year position at the Hun school concluded, I identified three possibilities that I seriously pursued, each one very different from the next.

One opportunity was an interim appointment with a school in suburban New Orleans. A second possibility was a position as director of the Phoebe Hearst Preschool Learning Center in San Francisco. The third choice was becoming the founding head of a new school, yet to be started, in Albuquerque, New Mexico. I began my trip in San Francisco, went from there to New Orleans, and then to Albuquerque.

Although I had earned a master's degree in child development and family relations and a doctorate in human development and family studies and had years of experience working with young children in schools and communities, Phoebe Hearst wasn't the right match at that time. It was limited to early childhood and was an art-based curriculum. I wanted a more comprehensive age range and a more inclusive program. The school in New Orleans wanted me to come back for a second visit, but I was drawn to Albuquerque after conversations regarding the vision for this new school.

I arrived in Albuquerque, New Mexico, in July of 1994 and met with a small group of founding trustees whose energy and enthusiasm were contagious. They had hired two consultants, John Bird and Len Richardson, who helped persuade me that I should take this opportunity seriously, that these folks were committed to seeing this happen, whatever it might take. That first year, we had no students, no parents, no teachers, no school building, and we had very little money. Getting things moving took an enormous amount of time, energy, and resources. We hired one other person, Cindy Groghan, and she became the office personified—business, admissions, administration, operations, and personnel. Cindy Groghan saved me by being an "everything" assistant. My job was to put a program together that reflected the mission, vision, and values of the school; hire a faculty who believed in and supported that mission; find families who were interested; and finally, open the school by the fall of 1995.

There were many people who helped make that happen, and that first group of trustees, led by Dr. Peggy Findlay, was simply amazing. They were, for the most part, parents of young children, and they were looking for another option for families in Albuquerque, perhaps with a different slant than the other three independent schools. Albert and Barbara Simms gave us office space in downtown Albuquerque, and Susan Palmer drove me around Albuquerque as we began our search for an adequate space. Three generations of the Simms family were deeply committed to independent schools in Albuquerque, beginning in 1938 with the founding of Manzano Day School, a highly respected pre-K–5 independent school, by Ruth Hannah McCormick Simms. Other schools to follow included Sandia Preparatory School, Albuquerque Academy, and the Bosque School. These schools represent significant achievements for *one family* on behalf of an *entire* community. The former Sandia School was the first to be established in the mid-thirties but had to close during World War II, and Barbara Young Simms was the person to reopen it as a girls' school in 1958 following the establishment of Albuquerque Academy in 1955, which was an all-boys school. All four schools are now co-ed and thriving.

At a board meeting in December of 1994, I advised the board at Bosque that there was enough money only to get through April and told them that if we were not going forward, I needed to know, so that I could start looking for another opportunity. I added that it had been a great experience, but the reality was that we had limited funds. After much discussion and the consideration of several options, the meeting ended. A board member came to me privately and said, "Your job is to get the school open. Our job is to make sure you have enough money. I will personally *guarantee* that you will. But I do not want the rest of the members to know that at this point in time." The money came from several sources, including the anonymous board member, but he did not have to contribute more than his fair share. And Bosque Preparatory School was born. Now we needed to furnish it.

While working at Choate Rosemary Hall, I had become acquainted with a number of other peer schools, including Deerfield, Andover, St. Paul, Taft, Exeter, and Hotchkiss. I called a few of my contacts, including people at Choate, and explained I was starting a new school in Albuquerque and asked them to consider donating old furniture they had in storage. I asked them to consider furnishing at least one classroom with desks, tables, and chairs (for both students and teachers), and if they agreed I would come and pick it up. The response in each case was positive, and they asked when I would be there.

I laid out a travel plan and then flew to Pennsylvania, where I picked up the largest Hertz rental truck available, a twenty-six-foot enclosed box, and made my rounds to various schools, loaded up the furniture, and returned it to Albuquerque. People pitched in to clean and refurbish the haul, and we were one step closer to opening a real school. If it were not for the hours and days of volunteer labor, it simply would not have happened. Entire families came to clean and paint, to build new walls, and to prepare for the arrival of our first students in the fall of 1995.

I interviewed a hundred teachers and selected eight talented and energetic pioneers who carried the weight that first year. They were excited to have the freedom to create and teach, and they used mostly original sources in language arts, social studies, science, math, Spanish, art, music, and physical education. On August 17, 1995, we opened the school to the ringing of a bell, a brass antique school bell that the Manzano School had given to Bosque. That same bell has rung every day since then for the past eighteen years.

For the first six years, Bosque existed in rented facilities in an older and somewhat vacant church facility near Wyoming and Menaul. Today the Bosque School, having shortened its name by eliminating the word *preparatory*, is situated on a campus of forty-five acres with nine buildings *in* the bosque near the Rio Grande. Now the name matches the location.

Bosque had been open for a year when Susan Richardson came into my life on August 8, 1996, in Santa Fe, New Mexico. I had been introduced to Susie through a mutual friend who thought we might have something in common. As I was going to Santa Fe to pick up some furniture, I called in a few days early and asked if she might like to go to dinner. She said yes. As the school was beginning to grow, we needed still more furniture, and the state of New Mexico had a division of surplus equipment that could be purchased inexpensively by legitimate nonprofit organizations, including schools. I told Susie that I would not be dressed very well, probably somewhat dirty and sweaty, and maybe not very presentable. She said basically, "No problem. You can take a shower and clean up at my house." Having never met, I was taken aback somewhat by her comments. She later confessed that she only said that because she knew I had been a Presbyterian minister. We went to dinner at the Natural Café, and she, knowing that I had been a minister, wanted to be sure to let me know her views on organized religion, because if we were in disagreement on that, as well as on other things, this was going nowhere. I listened as carefully as I could, considering it was our first date and I was nervous. I drank my second beer and said that I was relieved, that I had a lot of the same feelings and had pretty much left the organized church in 1969 over some critical disagreements about social issues that included civil rights and the Vietnam War, among other things. This seemed like a good beginning with more very interesting conversations to come in an enduring and ongoing relationship.

In 1998, Tony Gerlicz, an independent school educator, reformer, and charter school aficionado, and I put together the pieces for one of the first charter schools in New Mexico, the Monte del Sol Charter School in Santa Fe. Tony was the driving force and the "head learner," as he dubbed himself, for ten years, and the school received many awards and much recognition for its success and effectiveness with students. I was merely the founding board chair, and once again, it was my job to launch a project I believed would be important and worthwhile.

I learned back in the 1960s and 1970s that our public school systems, while working well in many places, were in dire need of reinvention to meet the needs of a legitimate twenty-first century education with a global perspective. And here we were in the '90s, and public education is much the same as it was 50 years ago. It seemed mired in the 1950s. I got involved in the charter school movement in the early and mid-1990s and continued my association and commitment to private, independent schools and their three-hundred-year-long tradition of preparing students for college and life beyond. We learned that the best teaching and learning practices involve listening, questioning, teaching for conceptual change, scientific literacy, metacognition, simulations, hands-on and minds-on learning, inquiry approaches, wait time, and real-life problem-solving. Research-based and data-driven decisions became the mantra of the day.

I worked with associations of charter schools in the early '90s in California, Arizona, Michigan, and New Mexico. Joe Nathan started the first charter school in Minnesota in 1992, and shortly thereafter, I was associated with the National Charter School Resource Center as a consultant. I believed then, as now, that it is possible to combine the best practices of independent schools with those of public schools and that the hybrid, charter schools, could meet the needs of today's students for the world of tomorrow. That model would be more efficient, more productive, and yield greater, positive results for both students and teachers. Charter schools have turned in mixed results, but enough have proven the point that a quality education can be delivered to any and all students if you have the best teachers and you understand the real issues in learning and assessment. There has been a lot of controversy and resistance regarding charter schools, especially from teachers' unions, as documented in the 2010 film *Waiting for Superman*.

The following year, 1999, I joined Carney, Sandoe & Associates, a search and consulting firm headquartered in Boston and serving independent and similar schools in the United States and abroad. Bob Sandoe started the firm in 1977, and Jim Carney purchased it in 1984. I worked with CSA and its clients for eleven years and enjoyed the experience immensely. During the next decade, I had the opportunity to continue learning how schools are organized and how those responsible for them lead and serve with distinction. I learned how things work well in many places, and how sometimes they don't, and what makes the difference. I concluded, early on, that much had to do with leadership both at the board and administrative levels. My work at CSA confirmed what I had learned in my earlier work as a teacher and administrator.

About this same time, I organized the Southwest Institute for Educational Research and Professional Teacher Development, a nonprofit organization whose purpose was to help teachers and school administrators explore best practices and their own professional growth and development. We conducted numerous seminars and workshops and had the advantage of being in a desirable location in Santa Fe, New Mexico. This nonprofit 501c3 organization became the fundraising and foundation for the Monte del Sol School, which then paved the way for organizing the Santa Fe Leadership Center in the next decade.

Chapter Seven

The Twenty-First Century and Beyond: Exponential Growth

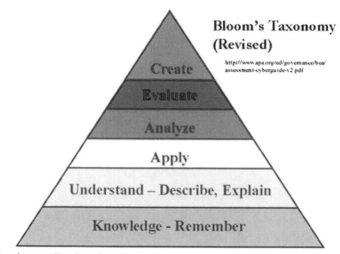

Bloom's Taxonomy (Revised)

http://www.apa.org/ed/governance/bea/assessment-cyberguide-v2.pdf

Create

Evaluate

Analyze

Apply

Understand – Describe, Explain

Knowledge - Remember

Based on an APA adaptation of Anderson, L.W. & Krathwohl, D.R. (Eds.) (2001)

I was able to continue my work with Carney Sandoe & Associates as a senior consultant and still live in and work from New Mexico. It required quite a bit of air travel, and we lived 110 miles from the airport.

After 9/11, air travel became much more complicated, uncomfortable, and inconvenient. My work was primarily that of an executive recruiter and school consultant, and with the advances of technology, I had the opportunity to be connected to the main office in Boston and with my colleagues and clients through the virtual world of e-mail, web conferences, Skype interviews, and some very fine resources and management tools. Significant administrative support made the work easier and more productive.

In 2007, while attending a national conference in Denver, a friend and colleague, Coreen Hester, who was starting her tenure as the head of the American School in London, asked if I knew of someone who might like an interim year in the UK at that school. I offered myself as a candidate for the high school principal position, and we moved to London in August of that year, staying not one but two years. I liked the school and the people there, and we loved living in London and the easy travel throughout Europe and the UK.

However, during the second year, Susie was diagnosed with non-Hodgkins lymphoma and had to endure some very serious chemotherapy that extended our stay by a couple more months. She received excellent care at both Princess Grace and Harley Street Hospitals. Dr. Leslie Kay, Susie's oncologist, was superb, as was the care demonstrated by the medical and nursing staffs from all over the world. She has been cured and thus far all follow-up reports have been positive and clear. We are enormously grateful. Susie is a veteran of survival. When she was thirty-seven, she suffered a subarachnoid hemorrhage (a brain aneurysm) followed by a stroke a month later. I continue to marvel at her attitude, her insight, and her deep understanding of health and mind-body connections.

This most recent decade may be one of unparalleled and exponential growth, especially in technology, largely due to the Internet and the ability to communicate globally and instantly. In June of 2000, there were ninety-seven million mobile phone subscribers in the United States. By the middle of 2010, the number had increased to 290 million. There are

Wi-Fi connections everywhere—at the local Starbucks and McDonalds, and also in airports, shopping malls, and some cities as well.

In 2004, there were one million subscribers on Facebook, and of this writing in 2013, there are over one billion. What explosive growth! Social media now includes many sites, such as Twitter, LinkedIn, MySpace, Google+, Ning, and numerous others. Rather than replacing embodied connections between real people, our devices supplement and extend them, creating an electromagnetic nervous system to match the physical infrastructure of transport built in the twentieth century—a network of connections, intersections, and switches. The big difference, of course, is speed. An e-mail can travel 10,200 miles in less than .2 of a second—.012 to be precise. That's the equivalent of 85,000 miles per second, 5.1 million miles per minute, or 306 million miles per hour! On the following page is a recent image of the world wide web from the Opte project. This project was created to make a visual representation of a space that is very much one-dimensional, a metaphysical universe. The data represented and collected here serves a multitude of purposes: Modeling the Internet, analyzing wasted IP space, IP space distribution, detecting the result of natural disasters, weather, war, and esthetics/art. This project is free and represents a lot of donated time.

A note from the creator, Barrett Lyon:

"The Opte Project was my first gift to the world and in the sleepless nights developing the software that traced all the routes of the Internet, I never thought it would touch so many people. Today the image has been used free of charge across the globe and is part of the permanent collection at The Museum of Modern Art (MoMA) and the Boston Museum of Science. It has been used in countless books, media, and even movies."

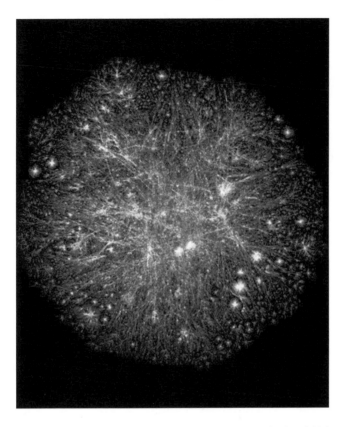

Oddly enough, after a decade of wild growth in invisible telecommunications, where one lived and worked mattered more in 2010 than it did in 2000. Travel and transport remained basically flat throughout the decade. Total vehicle miles driven, while an impressive three billion miles in 2010, were only up from 2.7 billion miles in 2000, even though the population had increased from 288 to 318 million, meaning the average American drove less in 2010 than in 2000. This was not true in my own case. For the past seven years, I have lived 110 miles from the airport and needed to fly frequently for work. I have driven many more miles in the past ten years than in the previous decade. For me personally, at this stage in my life, I much prefer the highway and byway travel to air travel, as do many other frequent flyers. Air travel in many instances is cumbersome, crowded, uncomfortable, and fraught with lines, an inept TSA, and unhealthy. Essentially, travelers are forced to breathe re-circulated air in a steel cocoon.

At 9:45 a.m. tomorrow morning, there will be roughly 4,500 commercial flights in the air, just as there were at 9:45 a.m. the morning of September 11, 2001. There has been no increase in travel despite a decade of economic and population growth. And mobility, the hallmark of twentieth-century United States culture, declined throughout the decade and reached a postwar low in 2010. According to the U.S. Census Bureau it was the lowest since 1948, with less than 10 percent of American households changing their addresses. That is still a fairly large number. My wife and I have changed our own area of residence five times in the past ten years. We've lived in New Mexico, California (one year), Oklahoma (three years), London (two years), and back to New Mexico. However, in spite of some moving around, we have owned the same home for the past eight years in Abiquiu, New Mexico and for us, that is home base. Learning to adapt to new communities, learning how to get around, finding the necessary resources, and becoming familiar with people and places are all essential ingredients to a successful change. In addition we have moved about freely in a recreational vehicle (RV) to many parts of the United States, Canada, and Mexico, spending as long as three months in Mexico.

At a Q Gathering in 2010 (events that explore the common good in a pluralistic society), urbanologist Richard Florida observed that young adults meeting one another no longer ask, "What do you do?" They ask, "Where do you live?" From what I have heard and seen, more people seem to be changing careers in order to stay in the place where they are, connected to family, friends, and local culture, than will change residence to stay in a career. The twentieth-century American dream was to move out and move up; the twenty-first-century dream seems to be to put down deeper roots. This quest for local, embodied, physical presence may well be driven by the omnipresence of the virtual and a dawning awareness of the thinness of disembodied life. My own preference reflects this trend. I came to New Mexico in 1994 and have stayed in the same region for most of the past nineteen years, far surpassing any other location in my previous life, except perhaps the first eighteen years of my life when I lived in one town and three different houses. There were those one- and two-year forays to other states and to the UK, but we always knew we would be returning "home" to New Mexico.

I moved from New Jersey to Albuquerque in 1994, then to Santa Fe in 1997, and eight years later, we moved to the country to enjoy a spacious and beautiful six acres on a river overlooking a mountain. Regardless of our preference for somewhat rural living, cities, the places where both connection and local presence can thrive simultaneously, experienced an extraordinary renaissance in the first decade of the twenty-first century. The revival of American cities was underway in 2000, but it reached its full flowering by 2010. Of course not every single American city flourished in the last decade, but those of us old enough to remember New York, Chicago, Atlanta, or Houston circa 1990, and others, including but not limited to Portland, Columbus, or Phoenix, can only be astonished at the way economically fading and often crime-ridden city centers have revived as centers of commerce and creativity.

The challenges often associated with urban life, meanwhile, had ignited a movement to the suburbs that may well accelerate in the 2010s. The frontiers of justice, mercy, compassion, and reconciliation are now in the suburbs, places where connections are harder to sustain and local culture is thinner and less appealing than the cities. Some suburban environments will reinvent themselves, but multigenerational poverty, crime, and gangs that provide a substitute social network where others have failed are already as common in Westchester County as in the Bronx, in the San Fernando Valley as in Compton. The most radical and difficult place to raise a family by 2020 may well be the suburbs, regarded by some as being their own ghettos of separation and isolation. A recent market study by a group in Philadelphia revealed a continuing shift in population as young families with young children are again seeking urban environments. What may be the most promising statistic highlighted in the report of social trends from the Pew Charitable Trusts, reflects what has been witnessed in cities nationwide: in a tough economic climate, many young adults are staying in the city, foregoing buying homes in the suburbs in order to remain mortgage-free. This has significant meaning for those who live and work there. I have learned that these young families would rather help create a sustainable community than spend an enormous amount of time commuting and transporting children along grassy, tree-lined streets from one place to another. While overall population growth continues to be concentrated primarily in the suburbs, there seems to be a shift taking place toward living where the jobs are, and those locations are in the more densely populated cities. Think about how often you hear people complaining about commuting to and from work and how much time it takes from their day. Now, think about walking to work or taking the metro and having more time at home, especially with family.

In the most recent decade, cultural majorities have collapsed almost everywhere. We learned that predominantly black neighborhoods became half Hispanic. White rural communities saw dramatic immigration from Asia and Latin America. City centers became internationalized. Mercados and Asian food markets sprung up in suburbia and in exurbia. Drive down a thoroughfare well beyond the 285 Beltway in Atlanta, and you will see shop signs in a dozen different languages. White Americans were still a bare majority of the population by the end of the decade, but in delivery rooms they were already only a plurality, the largest of many minorities.

We are all minorities now. Evangelical Christians are a minority, as are liberal Protestants, Catholics, Jews, Muslims, Buddhists, agnostics, and atheists. Barack Obama is a minority, but so is Sarah Palin. Republicans are a minority—so are Democrats and Independents. We now live in a country defined by its minorities, many of whom feel marginalized and no longer capable of wielding influence and power, but it doesn't keep them from trying. The most recent presidential election was a testimony to the vitality and importance of minorities and how some leaders connect better than others.

There may never have been a society in history that was as culturally, religiously, and politically diverse as the United States is today—except perhaps the Roman Empire. There are few models for how such a diverse community can sustain itself and plenty of models for failure. Perhaps the most hopeful model is a community that arose at the edges of that Roman Empire and eventually spread to its heart. In this community, there was "neither Jew nor Gentile, slave nor free, male nor female." This community, in case you don't know, was the Christian church.

That religious and spiritual community has survived, but its ongoing existence will continue to be a minority in a largely secular society, much as it has been throughout its history from the first century onward. I was part of that community in a professional role for at least ten years, and while withdrawing from it officially, I still find meaningful points of connection that inform, inspire, and sustain me personally.

I have watched the technologies of connection and the commitment to place define us into more and more tightly homogenous subcultures, refugees both virtual and real, from the heterogeneity of our society. Republicans became more Republican; Democrats became more Democratic, and the divisions became so fractious that any forward movement was paralyzed. Many people turned from traditional sources of news to the Huffington Post; CNN lost ground to Fox News, temporarily. In very recent times, Fox has lost much of its credibility due to their 2012 election reporting. A president elected on the premise of unity presided over two years of ever-sharper rhetoric of division and seemed unable to change the game. And then we hit the skids in 2008 and have yet to recover. It was not at all clear, as polarization accelerated, that anyone could convince any large number of Americans that they had anything crucial in common. My earlier vision of common or shared vision, values, and purpose seemed only to disintegrate further into oblivion.

When people in the next decade are trying to convey a picture of this most recent decade, they will use the self-portrait shot from a digital camera or cell phone held by one hand extended away from the subject. We look out at our own hand, perhaps squeezing another friend into the frame, composing our face in a smile or a laugh. We are shooting each other and, more recently, ourselves as well, as we learn of shootings on a weekly basis. An average of eighteen people per day have been shot since the massacre at Sandy Hook Elementary School on December 14, 2012, and gun sales have increased significantly since then.

I watched the visual presentation of the self accelerate in this most recent decade. We see ourselves most often in mirrors. But mirrors do not show us what others see—they show us a mirror image with right and left reversed. The difference is subtle but real, and symbolic of a deeper reality. Now most twenty-year-olds have seen thousands of images of themselves as others see them. They simply hold up their cell phone and click. In this recent decade, people have learned to shape and groom their image for public consumption. Body modification, augmentation, reduction, smoothing, straightening, whitening, and tanning, not to mention tattooing and piercing, have become normative. The closing years of the decade gave us the word "manscaping," which refers to male shaving, waxing, and smoothing to the point of unreality. That says a lot.

I witnessed another cultural shift from professional attire to casual. Men untucked their shirts, women wore pants, actually they have for a long time, and billionaires wore jeans. The most powerful CEO in America was universally known as "Steve." Indeed, informality was now a sign of privilege, only low-status workers wore uniforms. And the ubiquity of the camera meant that everyone, including celebrities, politicians, business leaders, people who in past decades would have been insulated by privilege, were caught off guard, meaning that status now accrued to those who could be most artfully informal, rather than those who could protect themselves from view. The paparazzi have contributed to this as have the twenty-four-hour news networks. The publicity-seeking individuals who want their fifteen minutes of fame add to the mélange of those seeking to be seen and pretending that they are surprised.

Most of the institutions where I have worked over the past fifty years had years of tradition, and they often struggled to stay relevant to an informal culture. Cable-channel comedians with open collars overshadowed tie-wearing network news anchors. Think of the differences between Tom Brokaw, Peter Jennings, and Diane Sawyer, as well as Jon Stewart, Bill Maher, and Steven Colbert. We can see how the journalistic practice of objectivity gave way to entertainment and sensationalism. However, Jon Stewart has a large following of those who believe that he tells it like it is with perhaps a little emphasis on the absurdity of so many situations. The best humor has often seemed to be the exaggerated truth.

Marriage, with its vows and formal attire, became for many young people a distant aspiration far on the horizon while cohabitation became the accepted gateway to adult relationships. Even among some of us in the older generation, a living-together arrangement (LTA) with a significant other (SO) was more than merely acceptable—it was desirable. In our case, our own children encouraged us to make our commitment to each other in public, which we did through a ceremony on a beach in San Diego with all of them present. We did that without benefit or burden of any governmental involvement, and it wasn't until we went to London that we had to make it "legal and official" with a piece of paper and a civil ceremony in a municipal court. Otherwise my wife would have been unable to stay with me during my time in London, but as my "dependent," she was granted a visa that accompanied my own work visa. I continue to learn the benefits and burdens of government regulations that impinge on my life much more than is comfortable. Many of these regulations certainly do not inspire confidence in the system— quite the contrary!

In the early 2000s, wealth was ever more disconnected from real assets. Countries that pumped black gold from the ground acquired vast resources of sovereign wealth that went looking for high returns. One of the most amusing and telling bumper stickers that I saw after our invasion of Iraq was "How Did Our Oil Get Under Their Sand?"

The most storied and prominent financial firm, Goldman Sachs, ended its century-long system of limited partnership and became a publicly traded company. Hedge funds made billions by trading not shares, but shares of bets on the future price of shares and derivatives far more exotic. Our mortgages, once the most boring and staid of financial instruments, were sliced and diced, traded and sold, and the housing market tanked in many places, making all that borrowed money subject to recall but rendering the price of the housing significantly less than what was owed. The term became quickly "under water" or "upside down."

As one Wall Street executive said, "as long as the music was playing, you had to keep dancing". As money swirled, prices of oil, food, housing, and labor spiked, then collapsed, then threatened to spike again. Those who could trade on volatility often made untold fortunes; those who actually needed to buy and sell real goods often suffered. What I learned during this period was that greed, corruption, and power could easily take us down the toilet while we sat helpless, watching the swirl in the toilet bowl. I preferred Gandhi's quote that, "there is enough for everyone's need but not for everyone's greed."

I observed another shift in business. In this decade, one of the greatest challenges facing leaders, such as CEOs of corporate and nonprofit entities, was managing complexity. Heretofore, the challenge was designing, implementing, and managing change. And change is still very present as a chief concern. However, we were now dealing with multiple, complex systems that required enormous investments of human capital to stay either on top or ahead of what was coming down the road.

One prime example is within the field of medicine, where there are at least sixteen thousand things that can go wrong with the human body. There are over six thousand drugs that can be prescribed to deal with these issues and over four thousand surgical procedures. To get it exactly right, at the right time, with a correct diagnosis and the precise and most appropriate treatment and accurate prognosis, is nothing short of miraculous and amazing. It's remarkable that it works as well as it does and as often as it does. That requires an immense amount of intelligence, understanding, and application of procedures all working together for the benefit of the patient. Similar concerns exist within other disciplines and fields as well, including my own field of education, although I believe we are woefully lacking in significant measures of reform and updating our methods and practices.

Yet all this complexity also contains the seeds of hope for a better outcome. The human brain, after all, is also complex, interconnected, embodied, improvisational, and is constantly being rewired. Simply put, it is the most complex system known in our universe. The culture of North America in the 2000s took several not inconsiderable steps toward embodying the same qualities as the brain. It was not without risks, not without loss, and with every expectation of grave difficulty ahead. And yet in the most surprising places, what was emerging could be called intelligence. Of course, intelligence needs to be married to wisdom— and in surveying the history of that most elusive of all cultural goods, wisdom, we can only conclude that the 2000s left us neither worse nor better off than human beings have ever been.

So what have seven decades of learning taught me to understand and to appreciate, to celebrate and enjoy and to use most readily in my profession and my work? I have learned most of all that life is about who I am, not simply about what I do. I learned that there is an important distinction between my work and a job. My work is what I care about the most, and my job is what I have to do in order to get to my work. My work has been with people, organizations, and communities. I have helped them to learn about who they are and how they can get closer to their dreams of the future. And what I have learned is that life is about *becoming*; we are always in process of becoming more like human *beings*, not human *doings*. What I do is about who I am. That means developing and growing our humanity, our human spirits, and being in touch and in tune with the natural world such that we not only *know* who we are and what we're about but that we place the highest premium on the sacredness of each human being, starting with ourselves. That yields tremendous results.

At the conclusion of the most recent decade, I have learned what works and what the critical variables are in the education equation. And it has taken me back to the beginning. I call it the full circle of success: common vision, common values, and common purpose. If we are to succeed in our schools and elsewhere in our country, we must learn how to build collaborative energy, listen carefully to what is and what is not being said, ask questions that are penetrating and honest, discern the real from the superficial, and help a group move forward with a purposeful, shared vision. That group could be your school or college, your company, your division, your task force, or wherever you find yourself at work. Hopefully you are following your passion and purpose beyond yourself. That is what has worked for me. I commend it to you for your careful consideration as you continue on your own journey of lifelong learning.